**The Polic**

CW00517026

Cabinet Books
Institute of Contemporary Arts

# Contents

*Cover: Proposal for a memorial for Mark Duggan made to Haringey Council by Tottenham Rights and Forensic Architecture. The circles, which were to be installed on the ground, indicate the location of the three elements at the heart of the incident that ended Duggan's life: Where he was standing when he was shot (the circle in the foreground); the location of the officer who shot him (left); and where the police said they found the gun (back). The proposal was declined in May 2021.*

Mark Duggan was shot dead on 4 August 2011 in Tottenham, north London. The shooter, a firearm police officer known by the cipher V53, was part of a thirteen-person undercover unit sent to arrest him. The national police watchdog, the Independent Police Complaints Commission (IPCC), misinformed the press about the incident, saying that Duggan was killed with a gun in his hand after he shot and injured an officer. Two days later, on 6 August, when the police had still not contacted Duggan's next of kin, Simone Wilson—the mother of three of his children—and her supporters in the local community marched on Tottenham police station, demanding answers and protesting ongoing police brutality and discrimination against Black Londoners. When the family's calls for accountability over the killing of Duggan went ignored, the protest grew into a confrontation with the police that challenged this status quo. From Tottenham, it spread quickly throughout England. The scale and force of the police response to this countrywide uprising against police violence were overwhelming; over the next four days, more than three thousand people were arrested. In what seems in retrospect like a path toward promotion, Boris Johnson—then mayor of London and now prime minister—presided over the police repressions, while the director of public prosecutions at that time, current Labour leader Keir Starmer, ran court sessions twenty-four hours a day to administer "conveyor-belt justice" to those who had been arrested, ultimately jailing fourteen hundred people.[1] Speaking in 2014, Johnson went further still, saying that the police should have "come down much harder" and gotten "medieval immediately on those people."[2]

\*

On 4 August, officers from London's Metropolitan Police received information that Duggan was about to pick up a gun from an address in east London. Driving four unmarked cars, the team began following the minicab in which he was traveling shortly after he had collected the gun, forcing the vehicle to stop as it entered the neighborhood of Tottenham.[3] Though the officers tried to get out of their vehicles before Duggan could leave the minicab, he managed to make it onto the pavement. The details of what took place from this point on—precisely in what circumstances Duggan was shot—are contested. Only about a second-and-a-half elapsed between Duggan's exit from the minicab and the shot that killed him, and yet this interval is one of the most controversial and consequential gaps in the recent history of London.

The shooting was not recorded on camera. The Metropolitan Police would require that body cameras be used during armed operations only following the conclusion, and as a direct result, of the inquest into Duggan's death.[4] The earliest videos—shot from a nearby flat and an overhead police helicopter—do not begin to capture the scene until after the incident. The police did have video cameras with them but only started recording once they began to administer first aid to Duggan, who at that point may no longer have been alive.

In 2018, Forensic Architecture was asked by the legal team representing the Duggan family to investigate the case in the context of the family's civil suit against the Metropolitan Police. When examining a scene of police killing, Forensic Architecture typically generates a three-dimensional model in which we locate the cones of vision from available videos—recorded by police-worn cameras or security cameras, for example, as well as by passersby—each of which depicts the incident from a different angle. Such models help us study what each video shows, what remains hidden between the various footages, and what the relations are between events captured by the different cameras.

The Duggan case posed a new challenge for us insofar as the evidence overwhelmingly consisted of words: verbal descriptions provided by the thirteen police officers, each positioned at a different location across the scene, and by the minicab driver. These are to be found among thousands of pages of documents, which include statements and reports provided to the IPCC and transcripts of evidence given at the coroner's inquest.

Our investigation focused primarily on examining the truthfulness of these testimonies. This required comparing the police officers' accounts with our models, and other material evidence, to show what they could and could not have seen at any given moment. Importantly, it also involved textual analysis, which entailed searching in the transcripts not only for divergences, differences, and contradictions between different accounts, but also for places where separate narratives converge so closely as to suggest the coordination of versions.

Though there were no videos of the shooting, each officer recounted the incident as if they were narrating videos that had been recorded from the position of their eyes onto the hard drives of their memory. Different officers described their gazes

| 1 | | a pivot movement and he's turned to face me. So at that |
|---|---|---|
| 2 | | time, if I could describe it, I'm in an off-aim |
| 3 | | position, I've got lovely peripheral vision over the top |
| 4 | | and I'm taking everything in. |
| 5 | Q. | Over the top of what? |
| 6 | A. | Over the sight. The weapon is slightly down, so I'm |
| 7 | | looking across everything so I'm trying to take |
| 8 | | everything in. |
| 9 | Q. | Had he actually parted from the minicab or did he have |
| 10 | | one foot on it or what? |
| 11 | A. | No he was out of the minicab. |
| 12 | Q. | How far out, do you think? |
| 13 | A. | I don't know, sir, not very far. |
| 14 | Q. | Okay. Then what happened? |
| 15 | A. | The only way I can describe it is like a freeze frame |
| 16 | | moment. You know, it's like if you've got Sky Plus or |
| 17 | | a video recorder, it's where you start pausing things, |
| 18 | | and in my head the world had stopped because as he's |
| 19 | | turned to face me, where I had lovely peripheral vision |
| 20 | | my focus turned immediately to what was in his hand. |
| 21 | Q. | How was he holding his hand? |
| 22 | A. | Again, may I stand up? |
| 23 | THE ASSISTANT CORONER: | Yes, please, yes. |
| 24 | A. | As he's turned to face me, he has an object in his right |
| 25 | | hand (indicates), Mark Duggan is carrying a handgun in |

45

*Excerpt from officer V53's inquest testimony, 15 October 2013. Image National Archives.*

anning, zooming, and focusing; most importantly, they spoke of their ability to pause their recollection and divide the incident into separate "freeze-frames." This meant that our prior experience of counter-investigating police brutality using multiple simultaneous videos could finally provide an entry point for assessing the possibility or impossibility of what was being described, albeit with two caveats: committing events to human memory is not as mechanical as transcoding them onto a tape, and the testimony of a police officer delivered under the threat of prosecution might not necessarily be faithful to that memory. This is not to suggest that videos present events objectively; they too produce their own biases in the way they are framed and edited, and even in the way different lenses distort reality in different ways.

While the incident was described from multiple points of view, the testimony of V53—the officer who shot and killed Duggan—is undoubtedly the "main shot." According to V53, he had a "lovely peripheral vision" of the scene once Duggan was on the pavement.[5] When he supposedly first saw the gun in Duggan's hands, his gaze, he said, shifted into "tunnel vision" and remained "focused" on the gun. To the lawyers cross-examining him at the coroner's inquest, V53 described his recollection in these terms: "It's like if you've got Sky Plus or a video recorder, it's where you start pausing things, and in my head the world had stopped." From one freeze-frame in particular, he claimed to have identified the gun well enough to describe it in detail: "I can see the handle of the weapon, I can make out the trigger guard, I can make out the barrel, and it's side-on to his body and there's a black sock covering that weapon." In describing that "split second"—a temporal duration he would invoke more than a dozen times during cross-examination—he testified that "I had an honest held belief that he was going to shoot me." After firing the first round at Duggan and discovering that, despite the shot, the gun was still "pointing towards my direction," V53 fired a second time and saw Duggan falling backward.

If V53's testimony described events as they actually happened, the gun should have been found next to where Duggan fell, mortally wounded. But it was not. It was found eight minutes later, and seven meters away, on the other side of a metal fence in an untended grassy area beside the road. Neither V53 nor any of the other officers at the scene could explain how the gun ended up in the grass. No officers said they had seen the gun being thrown, including the four positioned closest to Duggan, who asserted that they had not taken their eyes off of him at any time. This mysterious gap

in the narrative during which the gun disappeared was itself presented by V53 as if he were describing a vanishing act from early cinema, or as if one frame from the series of freeze-frames that made up his testimony had gone missing: "In the course of like a split second, one second the gun is there and the next second, when I looked and reassessed, the gun is not there."[6]

A character in a Jean-Luc Godard film famously said that "cinema is truth, twenty-four times a second." But the smallest unit of a film is not the frame alone but also the blank interval between frames, the omission of an image for a small fraction of a second.[7] And thus the gun that mobilized the entire events of that day in August—that initiated the original monitoring, the calling of the armed unit, the car chase, and the interception; the gun that purportedly had the eyes of the officers "glued" to it as Duggan exited the minicab, and which, according to initial reports, had shot a bullet at a police officer—vanished in the gap between two frames, only to reappear minutes later somewhere completely different.

After two years of being kept in police custody and forensic labs, the gun reappeared again, now presented as evidence to the jury at a coroner's inquest. It was at this time that the public learned that neither Duggan's fingerprints nor his DNA had been found on the gun. Yet after a four-month process, on 8 January 2014, the inquest's jury concluded that Duggan's death had been a "lawful killing."[8] The crucial question the judge instructed the jury to answer was: "Did V53 honestly believe or may he honestly have believed that at the time he fired the fatal shot, that he needed to use force to defend himself or another?"[9]

The legality of the use of lethal force was to be determined only in relation to whether V53 thought he perceived the gun aimed at him "at the time he fired the fatal shot." That the judge employed the term "at the time" is no coincidence. "Split-second" decisions are evaluated in relation to "the moment" in which danger is perceived "honestly and instinctively"; context, consequences, and retrospectively obtained information are to be put aside.[10] In asking the jury to render their verdict with regard to, and solely with regard to, this "split second," the judge seems to have himself employed the filmic imaginary existing in the law, one that divides time into discrete freeze-frames. That this imaginary was already embedded in the law might well have been the impetus for V53 to deliver his testimony in such a way.

*

One of the best-known references for thinking about the manipulation of videographic evidence in police brutality cases is the 1991 beating of Rodney King, a Black motorist, by Los Angeles Police Department officers. When the video of the incident—shot on a Sony Handycam by George Holliday, a nearby resident—was broadcast, it ignited widespread protest. The four police officers involved were acquitted when their lawyers developed a misleading, if innovative, visual strategy. Rather than play the video continuously, they chose to show a series of freeze-frames, decontextualizing each frame and allowing the officers to point to small movements by King —such as his body twisting in pain or him trying to regain his balance—as evidence of him "resisting arrest." [11] The video freeze-frames of the beating of Rodney King, like the mental freeze-frames of the killing of Duggan, cut these incidents out of a temporal continuity that includes their immediately preceding circumstances, their consequences in the future, and certainly out of the long-term history of police brutality against racialized communities.

The "split second" justification is a frequent last-ditch argument made by police forces worldwide whenever it might be demonstrated that they have used excessive force. In the US, this defense was enshrined in the 1989 *Graham v. Connor* Supreme Court ruling, where the court acknowledged that "officers are often forced to make split-second judgments—in circumstances that are tense, uncertain, and rapidly evolving." [12] Government agents taking such split-second decisions are, in most states, offered "qualified" or "good faith" immunity from civil liability. [13] In criminal trials, juries have tended to identify with the police officers and therefore accept many encounters as "tense, uncertain, and rapidly evolving," allowing for officers' errors and giving them the benefit of the doubt. A reliance on the "split second" defense is widespread; in addition to having encountered it in the US and the UK, we have experienced some version of it in our dealings with the legal systems of Israel, Greece, and Turkey. We have also encountered it from local politicians. Responding on LBC radio to Forensic Architecture's request that the investigation into the killing of Mark Duggan be reopened, London mayor Sadiq Khan said: "All I can say is that it was a tragic loss of life, but I'll tell you this, and I hope Londoners—and it's not a comment on Mark Duggan or what happened there—will understand this, but often police officers make split-second decisions, and we saw on Friday last week officers making split-second decisions on London Bridge. And they genuinely are split second." [14]

The "split second" argument is such a powerful component of defense strategies in cases of police brutality that it still needs to be invoked and even implicitly endorsed, if only to be rejected as not pertinent, when a case has nothing to do with instantaneous decision making. To take a notable recent example, Jerry Blackwell—one of the prosecutors in the trial in which Derek Chauvin was convicted of the murder of George Floyd—presented the nine minutes and twenty-nine seconds during which Chauvin slowly suffocated Floyd as precisely not a "split second" case. As he explained, "this case is not about split-second decision-making. In 9 minutes and 29 seconds, there are 479 seconds, and not a split second among them." [15]

The logic of the "split second" argument is entirely preemptive. It does not refer to situations of all-out confrontation, but to those supposedly pregnant with the potential for violence to erupt. In a split second, the officer must decide which of multiple possible futures is most likely to take place. A hand reaches for a pocket: is it drawing out a gun, a license, or a phone? Will the person shoot or stop? The argument cannot rely on evidence, as the threat never materialized. Rather, it takes the void left by the absence of objective evidence as to what would have happened had the officer not reacted and fills it with arguments about the officer's subjective sense of danger, or claims thereof. This fact makes it hard to convict officers against their word as long as they insist that they perceived a threat to their and others' lives. Police have therefore learned to call on the "split second" argument in justifying their deployment of lethal force, and the term, together with the filmic imaginary it conjures, has been invoked thousands of times in the US. [16] From the perspective of communities exposed to police brutality and murder, the "split second" is the most dangerous temporal designation: when it is invoked, one can be sure somebody has been killed or injured.

The split second thus becomes a duration in which killing might not be considered murder. The impunity and immunity it offers are reminiscent of the "space of exception" as conceived by Giorgio Agamben in relation to the concentration camp, or of the colonial frontier as described by Achille Mbembe, where the law, and in particular the prohibition on killing, is suspended. [17] Instead of suspending the prohibition on the murder of a particular class of people within a circumscribed space, the legal conception of the "split second" circumscribes this exception in time.

The precise duration of the "split second" exception has, however, not been specified. Is it a half, quarter, tenth, or thousandth of a second? In fact, the split second is not so much an indication of a span of time as it is an attempt, on the part of the law, to leave elastic the threshold of perception. It is considered to be the indivisible unit of legal time or the building block of human perception, analogous to the way a freeze-frame is perceived as the elemental unit of cinematic time. Both these durations black-box, and therefore place beyond legal judgment (or film criticism), anything that happens under their temporal threshold.

Though law hasn't done so, both science and cinema have, over the years, attempted to better understand the threshold of perception. In the nineteenth century, the duration of a "tenth of a second" was believed to be "the elemental unit of human consciousness," describing the lag between stimulus, sensation, and response time.[18] Cinema would exploit this duration in relation to "the visual threshold" needed for freeze-frames to "fuse and appear to move" continuously.[19] But just like different people may possess faster or slower response times, different sensitivities of film (or digital sensors) allow for different exposure times, which in turn are components in the enabling of different frame rates: cinema traditionally works with twenty-four frames a second and security camera footage ten frames a second, while professional video cameras now record at sixty frames a second.

In another investigation into police killing, we sought to better understand the components of this otherwise legally indivisible perceptual duration. The Chicago Police Department shooting of Harith Augustus, a barber in the city's South Shore neighborhood, was likewise defended as a "split-second" decision. Professor Tiago Branco, a neuroscientist from University College London, helped us dive into the scale of milliseconds by breaking down the killer cop's temporality of cognition, sensory transmission, and muscle response time. It can take between a hundred to four hundred milliseconds to parse and understand sensory input as evidence of intent, he said; a further hundred milliseconds or so are needed to process the crucial decision to shoot or not.[20] The faster the process, the more prone to bias it is. "Instinct," Branco pointed out, "is a short circuit to bias."[21] Once a decision is made, it takes approximately another fifty milliseconds for a message to travel from the brain to the muscles, and roughly fifty additional milliseconds for the finger muscles to contract and pull the trigger. The entire process of an extrajudicial execution

thus unfolds in a fraction of the duration that the legal process involving capital punishment takes to arrive at and implement the death penalty. And it weighs evidence, renders judgment, and enacts it not in relation to a crime a person has committed but to one that the police officer believed at the time they might.

Responses to a sense of danger perceived, as the law puts it, "honestly and instinctively" are described as if they were primordial and unconscious, as if they were the manifestation of a natural impulse for self-preservation. But police responses are learned, acquired through teaching and training. They are also culturally and politically conditioned, and prey to racial bias and political context. The probable future from the perspective of police officers will be determined to a large extent by their sense of fear and arousal, which might themselves be conditioned by institutionally engrained racist culture and dominant "common sense."

An exaggerated sense of fear is a constant feature in the long history of racialization. The brutal violence to which the colonized and enslaved were subjected was often argued as a matter of preemptive self-defense against the inherently violent nature of racialized people always about to erupt. To forestall their possible future violence, for which little evidence was ever needed, actual violence was applied in the present. As Marcia Willis Stewart, the Duggan family's lawyer, says in these pages, "Usually when there's a [police] encounter with a Black man, you hear that they're the strongest, most violent, most aggressive." It is in this way that within the "split second"—the molecular level of legal time—one could find the long durational history of colonialism and empire and the racist rage fueled by the sense of fear it provoked. Counter-investigating police use of lethal force, as this book aims to do, must try to look into the microscale of an incident, open the borders of its reductive temporal frames, and connect it to the world of which it is a part.

*

The jury in the Duggan case spent more than fifty days deliberating over the "split-second" moment and the issues surrounding it, and in the end accepted that "at the moment" V53 fired, he had an "honest belief" that Duggan held a gun. In a criminal case, consideration of self-defense does not require that such a belief be objectively reasonable, and the jury was thus never asked whether V53's belief was realistic in their view.[22] The question of how the gun got to the grass was secondary, though the jury accepted that "more likely than not, ... Mark Duggan threw the firearm as soon as the minicab came to a stop."[23] The jury's paradoxical conclusion that V53 could be believed when he said he had seen a gun that they themselves had deemed was not there could be taken to imply that, for them, it was reasonable enough for a police officer to imagine a gun in the hand of a Black person. Their ruling assumed that a racist perception was reasonable in these circumstances, unwittingly admitting that "honesty" was in fact a confirmation of racism.

A year later, the IPCC published its final report and offered a different explanation for the paradox than had the jury in the coroner's inquest, aligning its version of events even closer to the testimonies of V53 and the other police officers. According to the IPCC's findings, Duggan did leave the minicab with the gun in his hand, and was aiming it at V53 when the officer fired the first shot. V53 was not mistaken in his belief. The most likely explanation for the gun's position on the grass, they wrote, is that Duggan was in the process of throwing it when he was shot a second time. They believed V53 when he said he didn't see the throw, despite his assertion that his eyes were "focused" on the gun. Both the inquest and the IPCC dismissed another possible explanation for the location of the gun on the grass: that police officers had taken it from the minicab and planted it there. Forensic Architecture's investigation, as the following pages will demonstrate, arrived at the conclusion that this scenario is the most probable.

In 2018, Duggan's family launched a civil claim against the Metropolitan Police.[24] Whereas in the context of criminal law the police would be able to argue self-defense if they had an honest, if mistaken, belief that their lives and those of others were in danger, in the context of civil law, it would not have been enough for their belief to be honestly held: it also had to be reasonable for them to hold such a belief. This test is sometimes referred to as "subjective objectivity." "Subjective," because it regards only the information available to a police officer from their perspective; "objectivity," because it tries to assess whether claims for this perception could be supported by facts. As cases such as Duggan's move from criminal to civil trials, the weight shifts from perceptual psychology back to the material world. It was in support of this shift that the family's legal team approached Forensic Architecture to help spatially reconstruct the scene, otherwise obscured by a mountain of words.

Our investigation demonstrated the implausibility of both the inquest jury's conclusion that V53

could be believed when he said he had seen a gun in Duggan's hand and the IPCC's determination that Duggan was holding a gun when shot. (The former examined the officer's perception; the latter the presence of the gun). It also showed how the officers could have planted the gun in the grass, despite both inquiries discounting this possibility. The reconstruction and accompanying analysis that we carried out helped both interrogat the scene and reflect on the processes established to rule on the legality of the killing.

Aided by our report during pretrial negotiations, the family reached an out-of-court financial settlement in 2019, and Forensic Architecture subsequently worked with the activist group Tottenham Rights to present the investigation to the local community in Tottenham's old town hall. In February 2020, we met with members of the IOPC (the Independent Office for Police Conduct, the oversight body that has in the meantime replaced the IPCC) in our office to present our methods and findings, and then sent them our repor with the demand that they reopen the investigation. More than a year later, in May 2021—as this book was about to go to press—they informed us of their decision not to reinvestigate the case.[25]

In her response to the IOPC ruling, Marcia Willis Stewart, who represented the Duggan family throughout the legal process, commented: "Unfortunately, it appears that the courage required to confront and follow up the implications of [the new] evidence remains signally lacking in the IOPC today. ... Like the IPCC, the IOPC seems unable or unwilling to fulfil its responsibilities in relation to contentious deaths at the hands of the police. The consequence is ... that the IOPC lack the confidence of Mark's family and that of other families in their position."

Despite the IOPC's attempt to put an end to the case, however, the gun—both real and imagined, flickering between visibility and invisibility— will continue to haunt London, and especially the neighborhood of Tottenham, for years to come. □

Thanks to:
Stafford Scott
Raju Bhatt
Daniel Machover
Marcia Willis Stewart
Elizabeth Breiner
Robert Trafford

1. See Fiona Bawdon, Paul Lewis, and Tim Newburn, "Rapid Riot Prosecutions More Important than Long Sentences, Says Keir Starmer," *The Guardian*, 3 July 2012. According to the article, "Keir Starmer QC, the director of public prosecutions, said the speed with which rioters and looters were brought before the courts was far more powerful in preventing reoffending than the severity of sentences." Available at <bit.ly/3cnqasB>.

2. Mayor Boris Johnson speaking to the London Assembly's Police and Crime Committee on 29 January 2014. See Transcript of Item 3: Discussion with the Mayor on the Proposed Deployment of Water Cannon by the Metropolitan Police Service." Available at <bit.ly/3ipwqE6>.

3. Some members of Mark Duggan's family disputed the very fact that a gun had been collected. Forensic Architecture accepted the assumption of the Duggan family's legal team that a gun had indeed been collected.

4. See "Mark Duggan Death: Armed Police to Wear Video Cameras," BBC.com, January 2014, and "Metropolitan Police Officers Start Wearing Body Cameras," BBC.com, 8 May 2014. Available at <bbc. in/3FVEZ7M> and <bbc.in/34SKIdB>, respectively.

5. See "Inquest into the Death of Mark Duggan: Transcript of the Hearing 15 October 2013," p. 45. All further quotes in this paragraph are from the same document, pp. 88, 48, 45, 46, 50, 50, and 51, respectively. Available at <bit.ly/3g9vNvy>.

6. Ibid., p. 53.

7. In his 1975 lecture "Whatever Happens between the Pictures," Werner Nekes defined the smallest unit of cinema as the two-frame unit, which he names the "kine." Available at <bit.ly/3uTsD4o>.

8. See "Inquest Touching upon the Death of Mark Duggan," p. 6. Available at <bit. ly/3v0Ouqu>.

9. See "Questions and Conclusions Left to the Jury: 6 December 2013," p. 18. Available at <bit.ly/3pu3egC>.

10. This principle refers to anyone seeking to justify the use of force, not only police officers. See Lord Morris's comments in Palmer v R, (1971) AC 814 in the House of Lords: "If there has been an attack so that self defence is reasonably necessary, it will be recognised that a person defending himself cannot weigh to a nicety the exact measure of his defensive action. If the jury thought that that *in a moment of unexpected anguish* a person attacked had only done what he *honestly and instinctively thought necessary*, that would be the most potent evidence that only reasonable defensive action had been taken." My italics. For the US context, see Caren Myers Morrison, "Body Camera Obscura: The Semiotics of Police Video," *American Criminal Law Review*, vol. 54, no. 3 (Summer 2017).

11. See *Reading Rodney King/Reading Urban Uprising*, ed. Robert Gooding-Williams (New York: Routledge, 1993) and Thomas Keenan, "Watching without Seeing: Forensics, Video, Racism," a lecture delivered at the Sakakini Center, Ramallah, 6 October 2018. An earlier version of the talk, titled "Watching without Seeing: Police Violence and Eyewitness Video,"

was delivered at the European Graduate School on 22 January 2017. Available at <bit.ly/3g0vkwE>.

12. Graham v. Connor, 490 U.S. 386 (1989). Chief Justice William Rehnquist's opinion is available at <bit.ly/34WZwT6>. This case itself draws on Brown v. United States, 256 U.S. 335 (1921). In the 1921 US Supreme Court case, Justice Oliver Wendell Holmes made a ruling that would eventually become known as the "Holmes doctrine": "The right of a man to stand his ground and defend himself when attacked with a deadly weapon, even to the extent of taking his assailant's life, depends upon whether he reasonably believes that he is in immediate danger of death or grievous bodily harm from his assailant." See <bit.ly/3x69sFQ>.

13. The principle was first established by the US Supreme Court in 1967 in Pierson v. Ray, 386 U.S. 547 (1967). Available at <bit. ly/2TIWAqV>. Its current application relies on the 1982 Supreme Court case Harlow v. Fitzgerald, 457 U.S. 800 (1982). Available at <bit.ly/3uZFCS3>. The principle is also referred to as "good faith immunity" because immunity from civil suits is offered based on the officers' subjective state of mind and their claim that at the time of the incident they believed in good faith that their conduct was lawful, though (in a manner similar to English civil law) such belief needs to also be objectively reasonable. A good explanation of the principle can be found in Andrew Chung, Lawrence Hurley, Jackie Botts, Andrea Januta, and Guillermo Gomez, "For Cops Who Kill, Special Supreme Court Protection," Reuters, 8 May 2020. Available at <reut.rs/3pxTTnV>. The states of Colorado and New Mexico recently banned qualified immunity, while Connecticut, Massachusetts, and New York City have approved bills limiting it. See Nick Sibilla, "New Mexico Bans Qualified Immunity for All Government Workers, Including Police," Forbes.com, 7 April 2021. Available at <bit.ly/3cnIp16>.

14. Mayor Khan continued: "… but Professor Weizman, I understand the concerns that Mark Duggan's family and the community have and that's why the responsible thing for me to do is ask my deputy mayor to look into this new stuff, and see where it takes us." Some minor elisions have been made in transcription in the interests of clarity. See <bit.ly/3imHcuE>. The incident that Khan refers to took place on 3 June 2017, when three attackers armed with ceramic knives and fake suicide belts were shot dead near London Bridge.

15. See Andy Monserud, "Trial over Death of George Floyd Begins with Video," *Courthouse News Service*, 29 March 2021. Available at <bit.ly/2SZMOAp>. Blackwell's calculation was erroneous: nine minutes and 29 seconds is in fact 569 seconds.

16. In the UK, for example, it was employed in the very similar case of Azelle Rodney, who was shot, unarmed, in 2005 after a hard stop. The officer who shot him said: "There was no other way in the split second that I had to make up my mind to prevent him firing a fully automatic weapon and killing or seriously injuring a number of my colleagues." See "The Report of the Azelle Rodney Inquiry," p. 62. Available at <bit.ly/34WuGu4>. In Israel, Forensic Architecture encountered this argument

when investigating the 2017 police killing of Yaqub Musa Abu alQi'an. See <bit. ly/2T70bPr>. Gilead Erdan, the minister in charge of the police, explained: "I always back the forces sent on duty. … When we all sleep at night, they leave on hard and dangerous missions that require split-second decisions." See Michal Rotenberg, "Erdan Retreats," *Davar*, 23 February 2017. My translation. Available at <bit.ly/3fV0LZs>. More recently, we have encountered this justification in our investigation into the military killing of Ahmad Erekat. See <bit.ly/34Su4FE>. The government-affiliated NGO Monitor wrote that our investigation had been "unable to provide answers to the fundamental questions required to prove their assertions: What were the officers at the checkpoint thinking in the split seconds of the attack?" See "EU-Funded, ICC-Linked Al-Haq and Forensic Architecture on the Ahmad Erekat Shooting," 23 February 2021. Available at <bit.ly/3fXLbME>.

17. See Giorgio Agamben, *State of Exception*, trans. Kevin Attell (Chicago: The University of Chicago Press, 2005) and Achille Mbembe, *Necropolitics*, trans. Steve Corcoran (Durham, NC: Duke University Press, 2019), as well as Matthew Fuller and Eyal Weizman, *Investigative Aesthetics: Conflicts and Commons in the Politics of Truth* (London: Verso, 2021).

18. Jimena Canales, *A Tenth of a Second: A History* (Chicago: The University of Chicago Press, 2009), p. 15.

19. Ibid., p. 6.

20. Tiago Branco, interviewed by Forensic Architecture, 29 August 2019, as seen in Forensic Architecture's *The Killing of Harith Augustus: Milliseconds* (2019).

21. Tiago Branco, interviewed by Forensic Architecture, 29 August 2019. This segment of the interview was not included in the video cited above.

22. In their appeals to the Court of Appeal and to the European Court for Human Rights, the family tried to claim that the civil law test—that belief not only be honestly held but also reasonable—should apply. Both appeals were rejected. See Alexander West, "Lawful Killing … Duggan Revisited," *Albion Chambers Inquest Team Newsletter*, no. 6 (June 2017). Available at <bit.ly/3z7ixAi>.

23. See "Inquest Touching upon the Death of Mark Duggan," p. 3.

24. The family was represented by Marcia Willis Stewart of Birnberg Peirce and Raju Bhatt of Bhatt Murphy. Proceedings had been issued out of court in 2012 in order to safeguard the claim, bearing in mind the limitation period of one year applicable to any claim under the Human Rights Act 1998. The parties then agreed a stay pending the conclusion of the inquest and any ensuing challenge to that outcome by way of judicial review proceedings, which were finally determined in 2018 when the Supreme Court refused permission to appeal from the Court of Appeal—which, for their part, had allowed an appeal from a High Court decision to dismiss the judicial review. Consequently, the stay on the civil claim was lifted in 2018 and the family were then able to proceed with their claim.

25. The complete correspondence with the IOPC is available at <bit.ly/3pxUNkj>.

**Question 5**

When Mr Duggan received the fatal shot did he have the gun in his hand?

If you are <u>sure</u> that he did <u>not</u> have a gun in his hand then tick the box accordingly and then go on to consider unlawful killing, lawful killing or an open conclusion;

| 8 | We are sure that he did not have a gun in his hand |
|---|---|

If you find that it was <u>more likely than not</u> that he <u>did</u> have a gun in his hand tick the box accordingly and then go on to consider lawful killing or an open conclusion;

| 1 | We believe it is more likely than not that he did have a gun in his hand |
|---|---|

if you conclude that it is <u>more likely than not</u> that he did <u>not</u> have a gun in his hand then tick the box accordingly and go on to consider lawful killing or an open conclusion.

| 1 | We believe it is more likely than not that he did not have a gun in his hand |
|---|---|

Only if you are sure that Mr Duggan was killed unlawfully will you come to this conclusion and record it as such.

**Lawful killing.** If you conclude that it was more likely than not that the fatal shot which killed Mark Duggan was the use of lawful force – then you would return a conclusion of lawful killing.

**Open conclusion.** An open conclusion should be recorded when there is insufficient evidence to the necessary standard of proof for you to record any other "substantive" conclusion as to how Mark Duggan came to his death.

You may record an open conclusion if:

1) You are not satisfied so that you are sure that Mark Duggan was unlawfully killed; and
2) You are not satisfied that it is more likely than not that Mark Duggan was killed lawfully.

4. Conclusion of the jury as to the death:

| | Unlawful killing |
|---|---|

| 2 | Open Conclusion |
|---|---|

| 8 | Lawful Killing |
|---|---|

*Above: Pages from the conclusions and determinations of the jury at the coroner's inquest into Duggan's death, delivered on 8 January 2014. Images National Archives.*

In the early evening of 4 August 2011, officers associated with Operation Trident—a controversial police unit set up as an "anti-gang" force focused on London's Black communities—received intelligence that Mark Duggan, a resident of Tottenham whom they believed to be a member of a local gang, was preparing to travel to a location in east London to collect a handgun from a man named Kevin Hutchinson-Foster. The gun was one of a number that Hutchinson-Foster was storing at the house of an unidentified female friend.

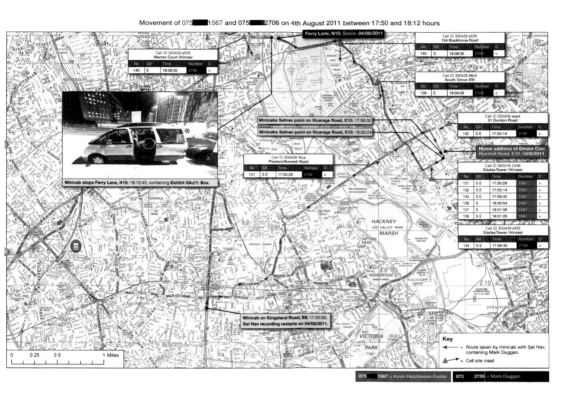

Having been aware of Duggan's interest in the gun for several days, Trident had asked CO19 — an undercover team from the Metropolitan Police's specialist firearms division — to arrest him once he had taken possession of it. As soon as Trident became aware that Duggan was en route to meet Hutchinson-Foster, they dispatched some of their officers to the address where the gun was being held. They arrived before Duggan, identified the minicab he was traveling in, and once they had confirmed the handover of the weapon, followed the cab as it headed north on its way to a housing estate in Tottenham known as Broadwater Farm. At the same time, the thirteen members of the CO19 team, driving four unmarked cars, were converging on the minicab as it made its way through an industrial area of northeast London, past open water reservoirs, across two canals, and approached Tottenham. As it neared a small bridge, the three lead cars of the team—which had by then taken over the pursuit—performed what the police refer to as a "hard stop."

*Above: Map combining data from cell towers and satellite navigation to trace the route of the minicab in which Mark Duggan traveled on 4 August 2011. All images in this section are from the National Archives.*

The first car overtook the minicab and turned left to block its path at an angle. The second stopped closely parallel to its right and a third blocked it from behind, while the so-called control car stopped a few meters further back. The nine officers in the first three cars jumped out of their vehicles to prevent any attempt to exit the minicab. However, the team was not fast enough and Duggan managed to get out onto the pavement, by which time three officers were closing in on him from both sides. The one known as W42, who had been in the passenger seat of the lead car, was near the front of the minicab, while V53 and W70, who had both been riding in the third vehicle, were approaching from the back. Duggan was in the middle, between V53 and W42.

*Above: An aerial view of the scene from a police helicopter. Note that by the time this photograph was taken, the CO19 team had repositioned their lead car so that some portion of it was on the pavement.*
*Opposite, clockwise from top: Detail from illustration produced by the Metropolitan Police identifying the locations of various pieces of evidence related to the shooting; CO19 officers performing first aid on Duggan; the open rear passenger door of the minicab, as viewed from a police helicopter, twenty minutes after the shooting.*

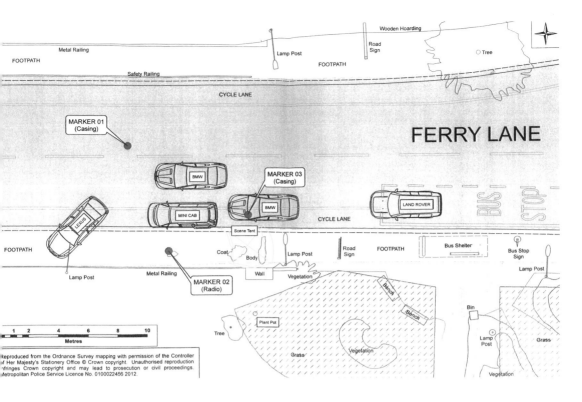

As Duggan turned to face V53, the officer discharged one round —a 9mm hollow point, or "dumdum," bullet designed to create maximum internal damage—from his rifle. The bullet passed through Duggan's right bicep and hit W42 in the radio he was wearing in a holster near his left armpit.

Duggan stumbled and V53 fired again; the second bullet struck him in the chest and exited through his back. It hit his aorta, resulting in catastrophic damage. A number of officers performed first aid on Duggan, but he may have already been dead by this time. Duggan was shot at approximately 6:13 pm; a doctor officially pronounced him dead at the scene at 6:41 pm.

When Duggan had collected the gun, it had been wrapped in a sock and placed inside a shoebox. The police later reported that the shoebox had been found open and empty on the back seat of the minicab, and V53 claimed that Duggan was holding the weapon—still wrapped in the sock—when he was shot. But according to the police, it was not until eight minutes later that they found the gun, lying seven meters away. Despite repeated forensic tests, neither Duggan's DNA nor his fingerprints were ever found on the sock or the gun.

The investigation that is the subject of this book assesses the feasibility of the various scenarios proposed by the police and the state as to how the gun could have come to its final position at such a distance from the body of Mark Duggan. ☐

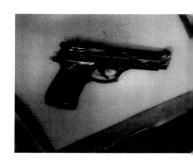

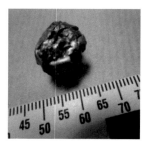

Clockwise from top: Police helicopter image in which the shoebox containing the gun that Duggan had collected is visible; the gun given to Duggan by Kevin Hutchinson-Foster; the bullet that hit W42's jacket and underarm radio; a photograph taken by a member of the public showing three uniformed officers and an unidentified CO19 officer near the location where the gun was reportedly found. The officers' faces were obscured for the purposes of the inquest.

## The Duggan Case, British Policing, and Colonial Violence: A Roundtable

Adam Elliott-Cooper, Temi Mwale, Sina Najafi, Stafford Scott, Marcia Willis Stewart, Eyal Weizman

*In addition to the many evidentiary issues at the heart of the Duggan case, the shooting should also be understood as part of much longer political and legal histories that have formed the ways in which British policing has surveilled and controlled Black Britons in the postwar era. The following roundtable was organized in order to examine these larger contexts. The participants include scholar Adam Elliott-Cooper; activist Temi Mwale, founder of the 4Front Project; activist Stafford Scott, founder of Tottenham Rights; the Duggan family's lead attorney Marcia Willis Stewart; and Eyal Weizman, director of Forensic Architecture. The roundtable, which took place on 9 February 2021, was moderated by Sina Najafi, co-editor of this volume.*

Sina Najafi: Adam, how far back do we need to go to understand British policing today? Do we start after World War II?

Adam Elliott-Cooper: It's useful to think about racism in British history not as something which arises in a multicultural Britain, after the Windrush generation arrives in the years following World War II and Black communities begin to be established here in the British mainland in significant numbers. It's more useful to think about racism as something that Britain exported to the rest of the world for a number of centuries through the transatlantic slave trade and the colonization of the Americas, of Australia, of the lion's share of the African continent, and of the Indian subcontinent and other parts of Asia. The capturing of that land, enslavement, the exploitation of labor, the extraction of resources — all required policing. And it wasn't the kind of stereotypical policing that we might think about today — the British bobby who's mainly only armed with common sense and a notebook — but a kind of policing fundamentally premised on a form of coercive violence necessary to control large colonized populations.

But the other thing that's important is that this wasn't simply a form of violence which used corporal and capital punishment, incarceration, forced labor, and ethnic cleansing. It was also something which was premised on racial hierarchy, on racism. Racism was, of course, really fundamental for justifying British colonialism in its slave colonies, but also, importantly, in periods of decolonization in the twentieth century as well. It's in that postwar period that we really begin to see the British mainland police being heavily influenced by forms of colonial policing practiced in places like Kenya, British Malaya, Trinidad, Guyana, or Jamaica.

There are three areas which I think can help us understand the police killing of Duggan. The first is the identification of a suspect community. In most of Britain's Caribbean colonies, this was often the working class and the trade unions, which the colonial police repressed; this can be seen, for instance, during strikes and protests in the Caribbean, such as the workers' movement in Trinidad in 1938–39. In places like Kenya, it was specific ethnoracial groups like the Kikuyu; in Malaya, it was the people of Chinese heritage; and in places like Zimbabwe, which was then called Rhodesia, it was the Black majority. And it's through the identification of a suspect community that you get the kind of stereotypes attached to that community: they have a propensity either for violence or criminality or deviancy, and therefore you need a form of collective punishment to be imposed upon this community.

This is really important as well, because in the colonies you don't have this clear differentiation between the police and the military. They're a continuum. You see militarized forms of policing across these colonies, whether it be the use of tear gas in East Asia and across the Caribbean in the 1930s and 1940s, or the use of firearms, torture, and mass imprisonment in places such as Kenya and Malaya. It's these patterns of colonial policing that start to migrate to the British mainland in the 1960s and 1970s. And it's in the early to mid-1980s that colonial policing really starts to come home.

I think this is partly because in 1982 Sir Kenneth Newman was brought in to head London's Metropolitan Police. Newman had been a colonial detective in the Palestine Special Branch before 1948, and later moved to Northern Ireland, becoming Chief Constable of the Royal Ulster Constabulary (RUC). He was awarded his knighthood for his work in transferring power from the British Army to the RUC in the 1970s. Additionally, consultants from colonial police in Northern Ireland and Hong Kong were advising forces across England in the 1980s, following the urban uprisings in places like St. Paul's in Bristol, Toxteth in Liverpool, Moss Side in Manchester, and Chapeltown in Leeds. It's through these uprisings, particularly in urban Black communities, that you begin to see militarized policing being justified to repress what were considered to be the inherently violent, inherently criminal, inherently deviant Black youth that resided in those localities. It's in Toxteth and Moss Side in 1981 that you see CS gas being used for the first time on the British mainland against citizens; before that, it had only ever been used in Britain's colonies in the Caribbean, Africa, and Asia. It's in the 1980s that you see for the first time — again in Toxteth and Moss Side — tactics such as armored vehicles being driven at crowds of people in a purported attempt to disperse them. Before that, you'd only ever seen it in Northern Ireland, and in Britain's other colonies. It's in the 1980s that you first begin to see baton rounds and rubber bullets being deployed, although not actually used, outside of Britain's colonies, as in the case of Broadwater Farm in 1985. This slow militarization of British policing wasn't something necessarily new; it was something very old to Britain, but it had simply never been used on the British mainland. It's the racist justification for this militarization which I think can help us to also better understand the context of 2011. Because by then there had been a continual — quite gradual, but

Top: British police guarding Kikuyu participants suspected of involvement in the Mau Mau uprising, Kenya, 1953.
Middle: The Fifth Pan-African Congress, held in Manchester, 15–21 October 1945. The speaker is John McNair, General Secretary of the Independent Labour Party.

Bottom: Overturned vehicle in Coldharbour Lane, Brixton, April 1981. The uprising in south London, which lasted from 10 to 12 April, resulted from the Metropolitan Police's use of "sus" laws to stop and question some thousand Black residents of the neighborhood in the five days leading up to the unrest.

Top: Crowds lined along Ladbroke Grove for the funeral of Kelso
Cochrane, Notting Hill, London, 6 June 1959. Cochrane had been
murdered by a group of white youths in the early hours of 17 May.
Middle: The British Black Panther movement participating in a
protest in Piccadilly Circus, London, against the British invasion
of Anguilla, 24 March 1969.
Bottom: Civil rights activist Darcus Howe addressing a rally for
the Mangrove Nine in Notting Hill, London, 1971. Howe, one of the
Mangrove Nine, was charged with "incitement to riot" following
a protest on 9 August 1970 against the police's continuous harassment
of the restaurant and its owner Frank Crichlow. All nine were
acquitted of this charge in the trial at the Old Bailey, which ended
in December 1971. Photo Horace Ové.

consistent — militarization of Britain's police as more and more police were being issued firearms and deployed on missions where they were allowed to use lethal force.

It's consistently racist ideas which are being used to justify this militarism, such as the kind of anti-Muslim racism that we have seen escalating following the bombings of 7 July 2005. But these ideas also help justify operations such as Trident, which was founded in the late 1990s explicitly to target so-called Black-on-Black crime in urban areas of England and Wales. (Scotland and Northern Ireland have their own policing policies.) It's this latent justification of violence and militarized policing that sets the real context for the killing of Mark Duggan and the rebellions which followed.

Najafi: What are some of the important clashes and acts of resistance in the history of how these racist police policies were imposed on Black communities in Britain?

Elliott-Cooper: I think there are probably three or four fundamental moments. If we're talking about the postwar period, I think one of the first and best known is in the late summer of 1958 in Notting Hill. It's in that year that a number of white vigilante groups attacked the homes and businesses of Black people living in that part of working-class west London. The attacks took place over a series of days, and you really see this come to a climax in May 1959 with the racist killing of a young man called Kelso Cochrane.

You saw there the complicity of the police and the state, either through the way they played down the fact that these were racially motivated attacks; or by ignoring the fact that these attacks were happening at all; or, more commonly, by claiming that this form of racism is an aberration, that it's something which runs against the norms of British culture, politics, and history, and that racist attacks are a stain on an otherwise pure and fair polity.

It's in 1959 that you see the beginning of real, organized resistance against this kind of racism, because activists such as Claudia Jones from Trinidad, who was a prominent member of the Communist Party, and a number of others, including Amy Ashwood Garvey, begin organizing around this particular killing. It's in this particular moment that such people begin to articulate, in quite coherent ways, that the British state, whether it be the Home Office or the police or other parts of the judiciary, aren't going to serve the function they claim they do. They're not going to protect Black communities from this kind of racial violence. In fact, quite the opposite; they are going to expand this kind of violence, and make it more pronounced.

It's from these movements in the late 1950s that you begin to see the emergence of what's generally referred to as Britain's Black Power movement. This begins to really develop in the 1960s with a number of different organizations, probably most famously the United Coloured People's Association, which kind of becomes the Black Unity and

Freedom Party, and the first branch of the Black Panther movement outside of the United States. Here, it's called the British Black Panther Movement, which, although it wasn't an official chapter of the US Black Panther Party, was in close contact with many of its activists and shared a lot of its politics — the politics of militant Black Power that we know today, influenced by Leninism and Maoist thinking, but also by solidarity with movements in places like Angola, Mozambique, Rhodesia, and South Africa, as well as other parts of the decolonizing world.

In relation to policing, the big crescendo involving the Black Power movement was the famous 1971 Mangrove trial in London. It's in the wake of a number of different campaigns that come together in the trial that you see this powerful confrontation between the Black Power movement and the British legal and policing establishments. The Mangrove was a restaurant in Notting Hill which had undergone a number of different raids and had a number of different cases of police brutality attached to it. It's in defense of the restaurant that you see a number of people arrested, some of whom then represented themselves in court, showcasing for the country and for many other parts of the world the way in which the police and the court system are complicit in the kind of racism which hitherto had often been portrayed as an aberration in Britain. And you also see a connection being formed between Britain's grassroots Black Power movement and Black professionals who were seeking to challenge and confront institutions of power in Britain. This included Black intellectuals but also those who were going into the courts and, rather than wanting to become part of that system, wanted to change it. It also included Black journalists and writers who wanted to make an important intervention in Britain's political landscape — they were unwilling to join and be absorbed into its institutions, and instead worked to develop independent Black institutions to challenge mainstream norms. It's within that particular culture that you begin to also see the ways in which Black Power in Britain was connected globally to a broader movement of Black Power in other parts of the world. I think that beyond those challenges to the institutions of the state and of the judiciary, it's the forging of international connections, as well as local ones, that makes the Mangrove Trial such a pivotal moment in British history.

By the end of the 1970s, you begin to see the decline of the Black Power movements, in formal terms, and a different kind of politics and different kinds of stories begin to emerge in the 1980s. I think Stafford and others can talk in more detail about the ways in which the legacies of the Black Power movement had a really profound effect on the people engaged in struggles in the 1980s, and how urban rebellion and revolts, as well as challenges within the judiciary system and to policing more generally, made the 1980s a really important moment for Black communities who were challenging police power and state racism.

Top left: The Mangrove restaurant, 10 August 1970.
Top right: Image from a pamphlet printed in support of the Mangrove Nine, 1971. Image National Archives.
Bottom: Police photograph of the demonstration in Notting Hill, 9 August 1970. Barbara Beese, who was to be charged as part of the Mangrove Nine, is holding the pig's head. Image National Archives.

*Top: Black People's News Service, published by the British Black Panther Party, July 1970.*
*Bottom left: Broadside in support of Tony Soares, 1972. Soares, a founding member of the Black Liberation Front and editor of its publication Grass Roots, was arrested on 9 March 1972 after reprinting an article from the US Black Panthers*

*newspaper that included instructions for making Molotov cocktails. He was found guilty on 21 March 1973 and sentenced to community service.*
*Bottom right: Race Today, October 1976. Darcus Howe was the editor of the magazine from January 1974 to December 1984. Image George Padmore Institute.*

Najafi: What were the mechanisms through which the various local organizations within the UK could share information and learn to articulate their various struggles? Were there conferences, for example?

Elliott-Cooper: There were a number of different ways in which people networked or shared ideas, which were obviously very different from today. One of them was international conferences such as the Pan-African Congresses, the first of which took place in 1900 in London. Probably the most famous one happened in Manchester in 1945, where you had people from across the African continent and the Americas coming together to organize for Black liberation across many different parts of the world. But you also had newspapers being printed and circulated all over Britain in the 1960s and 1970s — newspapers like *Black People's News Service*, *Grassroots*, and *Black Voice*, which were read all over.

One of the most important publications was a magazine called *Race Today*, which was founded in the 1970s and concluded in the 1980s. It was a platform for different activists who were involved in Britain's Black Power movement in the 1960s and who came together to really provide rigor. It wasn't simply reporting on news and providing the odd editorial; it was doing investigative journalism. It was going out and speaking to large numbers of people in places like Nottingham, where there were nurses who were struggling against discrimination and trying to unionize. It had a foreign correspondent based in Grenada when there was a socialist revolution there in the early 1980s, and in Mozambique when it had its armed struggle against the Portuguese in the 1970s. Having these kinds of global reports was really important, but it was also a fundamentally important magazine because of the ways in which it was able to report on the civil unrest that took place in Britain in 1980, 1981, and 1985, and the ways in which it pushed against the popular narrative that these were unthinking riots from unthinking Black youths. The magazine had people like Gus John going to community centers in Toxteth, Moss Side, and Handsworth in Birmingham, and spending time with the young people there and helping coordinate a lot of the defense campaigns that were being established. It enabled a far better analysis of what was taking place in the 1980s by connecting the kinds of intellectual work that people like Gus John and Darcus Howe were doing with the young people engaged in street battles and with the day-to-day violence of policing.

Najafi: Would others like to add anything?

Marcia Willis Stewart: I want to add to what Adam was saying about the communities that were not yet in Britain. In the early 1950s, many of the Caribbean islands weren't yet independent, and the communities there gathered to work out what they could do and how they could support their families in the UK. They weren't necessarily thinking directly of policing, but about how they could come together and voice their concerns around what was happening in the so-called motherland.

You have to remember that at that time, many of them were still part of the British empire, but of course the support for families in the UK waned, sadly, on independence. But it was very, very strong before then because people were coming to the UK to train as doctors and barristers and returning to their countries to fill key posts in all areas of government. There was still an investment in the people who were coming to the UK to be trained. And so they and those supporting them had a voice, and they used it.

Najafi:     Adam, can you tell us a little more about the politics of the particular organizations and publications you mentioned? How homogenous or diverse were they politically? Some of the publications you mentioned sound like they were leftist.

Elliott-Cooper:     It's funny, because a lot of the stuff I'm seeing on the news recently is asking if the current anti-racist movement in Britain is being infiltrated by Marxists. But the more I read about the Black Power movement in Britain, the more I realize that they were more orthodox Marxist than any of the young people that I've worked with today. I mean, these people were reading Mao, Lenin, and Trotsky. They were reading these Marxist thinkers in conversation with people who were thinking about a Black Marxism, a Third World Marxism — people like C. L. R. James and Walter Rodney, people in the United States like Stokely Carmichael and Angela Davis.

All these different types of Marxists would have had big arguments about who was correct, but what is important is that they all understood that racism is fundamentally linked to capitalism and to a class system. They weren't simply trying to recreate the world as we currently know it, with some Black FTSE 100 companies and some Black politicians in Parliament, with the same kind of class hierarchies that exist but with a multiracial class hierarchy. They wanted to do away with both racial and class hierarchies.

The second thing that's really important about their politics is that they were anti-imperialist. They understood racism was not about prejudice and people not liking people who they deemed to be outsiders for one reason or another. They understood racism as being fundamentally linked to exploitation and profit, to the extraction of resources and the taking over of lands. By understanding racism in its global context, influenced by the thinking of people like Mao, as well as Walter Rodney, C. L. R. James, and people like that, they were able to understand that they had to think internationally even while they were always working directly with the grassroots.

I think that was a really important part of their politics, a politics that I think a lot of people in the current generation could learn from in understanding the importance of not only class but also internationalism.

Najafi:    Stafford, would you pick up the story from the 1980s, which is not only an important threshold moment but also when you became involved in activism?

Stafford Scott:    I'm a child of the 1960s. My generation is in many ways the generation that doesn't get spoken about that much. We are the children of the Windrush generation; we are the very first generation born in this country "en masse," the first generation to go into the education system "en masse." That's how they perceived us back then.
The community lived in specific localities in those days. Initially, most of our communities, especially the Jamaican community, would have been located in Brixton, and obviously, we had communities in Ladbroke Grove. In north London, we were in Stoke Newington to begin with, and then we came to Tottenham. When my generation entered the education system, our numbers in the schools in our areas may have appeared to be a bit disproportionate compared to the rest of the country. They said we were swamping the education system. It was an education system that wasn't ready for us, an education system that we feel treated us particularly badly.
Today, I saw a professor, Sir Geoffrey Palmer, on television. For those of us who know his story, he's a cult figure in our community. He was a character who came to this country from the Caribbean as a teenager in the 1950s. He was put into a so-called ESN school, a school for the educationally subnormal. Black children were being put into these schools disproportionately as a means of getting us out of the mainstream education system. Sir Geoffrey went on to become one of this country's foremost scientists. He's a professor emeritus based in Scotland. He only became this great professor because when he was sent to a school for educationally subnormal children, he was found to be a great cricketer. So they took him out of that school and sent him to a normal school, a private school, and he was allowed to reach his full potential.
The rest of us were never given those kinds of opportunities. We were violated in the education system. And by the time we came out of that education system "en masse," there'd been a downturn in the fortunes of this country. Our parents had been invited over to help rebuild the country post-World War II. By the time we were coming through the education system in the early 1970s, economic decline meant that the jobs that they invited our parents here to do, the jobs that the English didn't want to do themselves, were no longer available to us.
We weren't felt to be good enough. We didn't have any spaces or places, any community centers or halls or clubs where we could gather. As young people, we ended up taking to the streets. We started to come together, to self-support to resist racist attacks and racist policing. We started to listen to the culture coming from Jamaica. We laugh nowadays; we say, white people like Bob Marley now. We would listen to Bob Marley, but we weren't listening to "Three Little Birds." We were listening to "War": "Until the philosophy which

hold one race superior, and another inferior, is finally and permanently discredited and abandoned, everywhere is war."

We saw all the things that Adam told you were there in our community in our parents' generation. We were being told, for example, that an Englishman's home is his castle, yet we saw police officers just walk into our parents' castles and treat them as they wanted. We decided we were going to resist these kinds of behaviors and in response, the police began to use what are called the sus laws, "sus" standing for "suspected person." It's an old law that had been on the statute books, but they'd stopped using it. They started to use these laws against young Black people to stop us from being able to congregate or being able to move around freely, and in so doing they criminalized large swaths of the young Black community.

It was so bad that they had institutions called detention centers and borstals in which they would lock young, predominantly Black kids up using the sus laws. In 1981, the uprisings that happened in Brixton were a result of the police — the same officer that Adam spoke about, Kenneth Newman — using the sus laws in that one particular geographical location. It was called Operation Swamp, and they literally stopped every Black kid over a certain age to arrest them using the sus laws. That ended with uprisings and then with the Scarman Inquiry, which ended the sus laws. But those laws really criminalized and penalized us and meant that we couldn't go forward in terms of careers in a system that didn't want us in the first place.

To understand the sus laws: police officers could take us to magistrates' court and say that they had seen us behaving in a suspicious manner. They didn't need a victim or witnesses. You can imagine how that was used against us. The first thing I was ever arrested for in my entire life was "sus." And if I told you the story, you'd understand it wasn't a case of mistaken identity; the crime itself did not happen.

What it meant for us as young Black kids is that we felt that we didn't have a place in this society. Adam has painted a wonderful story of our parents' struggles, but unfortunately their struggles didn't come to anything that was material, so we also felt we were being let down by our parents. We felt that international struggle was a struggle that needed to happen, but we felt that it was a struggle where they needed to support us, because we were here in the belly of the beast. We became a very inward-looking community. We're mainly now talking about those who were born here and those who came here at a really young age. There's a real Black British experience, and for us, it was really a Jamaican vibe, through music and such.

The UK, apart from issues of race, was a pretty liberal society. They were stopping things like corporal punishment, but in our homes corporal punishment was the norm. We were still getting a Caribbean kind of treatment from our parents, post-traumatic slave syndrome and such. So we had to rebel and resist. For us, the institutions were run by racists and our homes were run by mad people. We were being squeezed in the middle. We couldn't come home and tell our parents that a cop had stopped us. "Why did he stop you?" "Because he's a racist."

"You must have done something." "*Hello*, we were walking whilst being Black." So, we had difficulties with our parents. We had to educate them to understand what racism truly meant. Because of the time we were born, my generation has a perspective on racism that most other Black communities, apart from maybe in America, are still yet to develop.

In north London, in Haringey, we were just then getting to that age where people want to leave their parental homes. Many in my generation went to Haringey Council for assistance when looking for housing. I was fortunate not to be in this group, but they went to the council, and the council housed them on a rundown, hard-to-let estate called Broadwater Farm. The council had adopted what was later identified by Lord Gifford, in the public inquiry that followed the 1985 uprisings, as an institutionally racist housing policy. And they put large numbers of youths onto this estate.

That changed the makeup of the estate. It was just young Black youths and older white people — not even families, but older white couples who had been trapped on the estate and couldn't get off. The estate was also architecturally designed for crime. It really was. It was built on stilts, lighting was terrible, and there were long corridors. There would be fifteen flats in one corridor, and people worked out that if you broke into flat number one, you could go through fire exits that led into the other flats. So you broke into flat number one, and you could rob fifteen flats if everyone was out. The estate became a mad hotbed of crime. As a consequence, the police said they wanted to open a police station on the estate. And we said, "No, you can't do that because you're only going to further criminalize the youths."

I was a youth worker at the time — the youth I was supporting was my generation, my friends, my peers. With the support of a woman called Dolly Kiffin, we came together and formed the Broadwater Farm Youth Association. We said to the council, "You can't allow the police to open a station on this estate. It's going to lead to uprisings and to the criminalization of our community, and what we want is an opportunity to be able to work with our young people, to empower them, so that they can start to deliver services to other young people on the estate who look like them." At the time, with the support of Bernie Grant, we were able to build and grow and deliver services, not just to young Black people, but to the rest of the estate.

Najafi:  Who was Bernie Grant?

Scott:  He was the first Black leader of a municipal authority. The reason he became leader of Haringey Council is because he threw a coup after the council allowed the National Front — that was the big fascist organization — to hold a meeting in one of its schools. Bernie was very supportive of us Black youths in the community. So as our youth association started to deliver services not only to our community but to the wider community, others saw that we'd got rid of the few racists around and created a safe space. It meant that most Black people who lived in this area started to come to Broadwater Farm; they didn't have to have anything to do with the estate. They just came there to be recipients of the services and to feel part of a community that wasn't under the constant cosh of the police. It was a great place to be. We loved it, until October 5th, 1985, when the police arrested Floyd Jarrett, claiming he had stolen a car because he was driving what was a mashed-up BMW. The stereotype was that we shouldn't be driving those kinds of cars, and the actions after that led to the death of his mother, Cynthia. They also led to what we now know as the Broadwater Farm uprisings, in which policeman Keith Blakelock lost his life.

There's a strong belief in our community that we've been paying for that day ever since. When Kenneth Newman came to London, he identified Broadwater Farm as one of the symbolic locations for policing across the city. We didn't understand what he meant when he said it at the time, but "symbolic policing" meant that we were going to be overpoliced from then on.

As a result, we had the uprising on October 6th, 1985, when Blakelock lost his life. We had six of our community members arrested and charged with his murder. At the trial at the Old Bailey in March 1987, three of them — now known as the Tottenham Three — were sent to prison for life. In 2001, we had the appeal, where the court found that Winston Silcott, in particular, had been framed, and the three men were acquitted and released.

Najafi: Can you talk a little bit about the death of Cynthia Jarrett?

Scott: Floyd Jarrett was a senior member of the Broadwater Farm Youth Association. He was driving home when three police officers stopped him, and said that he was driving with an out-of-date tax disk. It turned out that that was not the case. They then arrested him because they claimed that he had tried to assault them. They took him to the station, and an off-duty police detective called Mike Randall saw him being brought in and identified him as a senior member of the youth association. Instead of going home, this officer decided to get involved. He took Jarrett's keys and together with three other officers went to the family home, though Jarrett didn't live there. He opened the door with the keys; he didn't ring the bell and announce himself. They went inside and the mother who was there with her daughter and grandchild was shocked when she saw these white men in her home. Randall then pushed her over as he went about the raid. She fell to the floor and basically didn't ever recover.

He stepped over her on the way out. When outside, he radioed the station and said that everything had gone fine. She was in there dying from a heart attack. The finding at her inquest was it was an "accidental death." The coroner was clear that "accidental death" meant that the jury would have had to accept that the police officers touched her and caused her to go to the ground, even though the police have never accepted it. The police didn't follow up on the judge's ruling that they should consider the possibility of disciplining the officers involved, so we were particularly angry at what happened to her, but I need to contextualize it. Exactly one week before, back in Brixton, the police had shot a Black woman, Cherry Groce. They had gone to her home looking for her son Michael. She opened the door, saw armed police officers, turned to flee up the stairs in her nightdress, and they shot her in the back. They crippled her, and eventually the bullet they put inside her body was to kill her. In Tottenham, we were particularly upset hearing that. What was also going on at the time was a power struggle in South Africa. We had Soweto and Sharpeville and we lived those lives with our South African brothers and sisters. All of a sudden, it was happening on our doorstep, with a Black mother shot. There were uprisings in Brixton that weekend. So when, on the following weekend, they went a step further and took the life of a Black mother, an uprising was almost certain to happen. We on Broadwater Farm wanted to go to the police station to demonstrate and to demand that they suspend the officers involved in the raid on Cynthia Jarrett's home. The police tried, we believe for the first time, to kettle an entire estate and trap us there, to deny us our right to demonstrate, so that our voices couldn't be heard. You know what Martin Luther King says about what happens when a community cannot have their voice heard; it makes itself heard in different ways.

Since then, we've had the death of other community members. Joy Gardner was killed on August 1st, 1994. She was forty. She was killed in the most horrific of circumstances. Officers from the Home Office and the police entered her home. The crime that she had committed was overstaying in our wonderful country. They put handcuffs on her hands and manacled her feet. They sat on her and did God knows what else to her, and she died. They wrapped fourteen feet of masking tape around her mouth and nose. They did it whilst her five-year-old son was in the corner watching. He was just committed to a psychiatric hospital the other day, by the way; we live with the trauma caused by their behavior.

In January 1999, they killed Roger Sylvester, also a member of the Broadwater Farm Youth Association. Six police officers took him from his home and ... we saw what they did to George Floyd the other day, and that's what they did to Roger Sylvester. They told us that he died of ... is it called combustible delirium, Marcia? That he got himself into such a whir — this only happens to Black people and it only happens to us when we come into contact with police officers — that he just blew up.

Willis Stewart: It is referred to as "excitable delirium," but you're right to think of it as combustible, because that's what they want to convey with the term.

Scott: We had to wait about four years for an inquest. It took months to hear all the evidence and the jury took two hours to say "unlawful killing." The judge then dismissed and overturned the verdict; he said that he believed the jury was confused. They changed the law as a result of all this. After that case, they stopped putting the option of "unlawful killing" in front of inquest juries, and brought in the notion of what they call a "narrative verdict."

Then, in 2011, we had the killing of Duggan. I think the Forensic Architecture model says everything we need to say about that, apart from the callous, inhumane way they treated the family before and during the investigation. Then the one that we don't talk about so often; the killing of Jermaine Baker on December 11th, 2015, at the age of twenty-eight. You see that the age is getting younger and younger every time they take the life of someone in our community.

Najafi: You said that that at some point the sus laws were suspended, but it seems that some version of what in New York is called stop-and-frisk did continue to be used in the UK. Is that correct? Is it the case that the police just devised a new method for doing essentially what the sus laws had done?

Scott: Absolutely. When I was growing up, we didn't have stop-and-search because police officers had to take you to a station if they wanted to search you. We had the sus laws. When we managed to bust the sus laws, that's when they started stop-and-search. It shows that the police have to have an instrument to control our ability to move, our sense of freedom, an instrument where they can treat us in a way that belittles and controls us at all times.

Weizman: I know Stafford's work on the police's Gang Violence Matrix database and I wonder, Stafford, if you think that the preemptive or predictive logic of the sus laws — it's not what you have done but what you will have done — is somehow related to the predictive logic of the Matrix?

Scott: Absolutely. It's one continuum.

Najafi: What is the Matrix?

Scott: Let's come back to the Matrix when we talk about the events of 2011. It was the government's response to the riots in Tottenham and across the UK that followed the killing of Mark Duggan.

Najafi: Let's move to 2011. Marcia, could you tell us about the important legal issues in the case?

Willis Stewart: First, I want to go back to a couple of things that Stafford said. He mentioned being caught between what was happening outside and inside the home. There has to be an understanding of how the Black community was othered, and then how that community itself further marginalized those who wouldn't "conform" within it. Young people, as Stafford said, couldn't go home and tell their parents that they'd been stopped by the police or that they'd had difficulties at school from either a teacher, children in the class, or in the playground because of the perception that it must have been them that had done something bad.

Going back to the sus law, this was a stop-and-search law that permitted a police officer to stop, search, and potentially arrest people on suspicion of them being in breach of section 4 of the Vagrancy Act of 1824.

Another piece of old legislation that has been used is "joint enterprise." Adam talked about the relationship with the colonial past, and we see where bits of old colonial legislation are brought in to control and to create a situation where there's further scope for punishment.

Najafi:  What is joint enterprise?

Willis Stewart:  Joint enterprise is a common law doctrine where an individual can be jointly convicted of the crime of another, if the court decides that the person could see, expect, or predict that the other party was likely to commit that crime. It is used, for example, where a group of young people are out and an individual gets stabbed and you can't say who the perpetrator was. There have been a lot of challenges to joint enterprise; the Prison Reform Trust have been doing a lot of work, and an activist group called JENGbA (Joint Enterprise Not Guilty by Association) has been campaigning on the issue.

Speaking of Roger Sylvester, I came home one weekend in 2016, and at the top of my road, I heard screaming. There were two police officers; one had a man face-down with his knee on his neck, and another was trying to cuff him. The man was saying, "I can't breathe." I shouted, "Stop that right now." The police officers looked at me and told me to go away. And I said, "Stop it right now." Still nothing. And then I said, "Do you want a repeat of Roger Sylvester?" At which point the officer said to me, "That's not very helpful, ma'am." I said, "Haven't you heard of postural asphyxia? You sit him up right now." It was important to intervene; I was concerned not for myself but for the man, who was clearly distressed and, more importantly, was having difficulty breathing.

The question is often asked: "What can you do when you see these things happening?" My response is, and this is not just the responsibility of Black people: anyone seeing this should stop and observe. It is sometimes necessary to make your presence known by asking what the problem is. Officers need to be aware of your presence. You do however need to make sure you do not place yourself at risk. Sometimes the easiest thing is to shout out, making your presence known. This isn't about breaking the law — it might simply be about saving a life.

Najafi:  Do people use cell phones to record such incidents as extensively in the UK as they do in the US? And what is the legal status of filming the police?

**Willis Stewart:** Film the incident if you can, or make an audio recording on your phone. Whatever you do keep a copy. Don't just hand over your phone.

**Temi Mwale:** A common tactic that the police use is to say that even filming them is "obstructing." When we run police interaction training for our staff and young people, we make sure to emphasize how important it is to film. We tell them to make sure they are at a distance so that the police can't say, "You're obstructing." Many officers even say, "You're not allowed to film," but that's not the law. We see that young people are particularly harassed when trying to assert their rights, and being told that there's already a body camera. But the police-worn body cameras are facing the wrong way! We've had young people's phones chucked to the ground, luckily still recording, but now you can't see anything. Or police officers just confiscating their phones, and some of those phones have not been given back. The more that young people assert their rights and community workers observe what's happening and try to intervene, the more they are obstructed with the claim that they themselves are obstructing.

    And it's very difficult to get hold of the body-cam footage, even when you make sure you ask for it to be saved. Sometimes, it takes a very long time for it to be provided, if at all. In some cases, when we haven't been able to film, we've even had lawyers on FaceTime live-watching what is happening and saying, "I'm a lawyer, I'm watching you." But even that doesn't seem to prevent abuses from taking place.

    We must film; they know how powerful it is to have records other than their own cameras. We fought for body cameras; it's progress, but they can just turn them off. Nobody talks about how useful body cameras really are when they can just do that.

**Willis Stewart:** When I speak to people who are older, I say to them, you have a responsibility to record either by filming or taking a note. I also suggest that they get somebody to film the person filming. If this is not possible, it might be helpful to telephone someone you trust and let them listen to what's going on. The point is to not put yourself in danger, and certainly there are often efforts to prevent filming. The point is to make a record of what you've seen in the best and safest way possible.

**Najafi:** Was the complete lack of body cams in Duggan's killing unusual at that time?

**Willis Stewart:** It was very unusual. In a nation where surveillance is part of everyday life, it was incredible that there was no surveillance on that stretch of Ferry Lane. It was incredible how little footage there was. In fact, the only footage was that of the resuscitation efforts and from the person filming from the flats.

**Najafi:** Can we talk about the case from a legal perspective — the coroner's inquest, the Independent Police Complaints Commission (IPCC) report, and the civil suit? I was very surprised to hear that the IPCC report was in part relying on evidence gathered by the same police who they were investigating. Was there a separate, independent gathering of evidence from the scene?

Willis Stewart: The IPCC gathered the evidence because it was their mandate to investigate this fatality. Although the Metropolitan Police were not in control of the IPCC investigation — so, yes, the investigation was "independent" of the Metropolitan Police — the IPCC did not have the resources to carry out independent forensic examinations, so these investigations had to go through the police service. And the IPCC's officers were often former police officers, retired either from the Metropolitan Police or other forces.

Najafi: What repercussions did this lack of independence have for the case?

Willis Stewart: Initially, it was unclear as to which organization was in control, and for the family there were conflicting messages, i.e., what was the role of each organization. So, for example, the family were not informed that Mark had been shot and they had to rely on press announcements for information. The Metropolitan Police should have informed the family that Mark had been fatally shot — it was their responsibility. It was the role of the IPCC to begin an immediate and unbiased investigation, as opposed to relying on the erroneous press statements, etc. The IPCC should not have relied on information provided by the police regarding "an exchange of fire," which led to an inaccurate account of an "officer being shot."

The fact that investigating officers in the IPCC were former police officers meant that the family felt that, more often than not, it was Mark being investigated, as opposed to the officers involved in the operation which resulted in his death. The investigating officer was extremely surprised after the forensic results, which showed that Mark's DNA was not on that gun. Try as they could, they couldn't get around that fact. Significant resources were expended trying to prove, rather than disprove, that Mark's fingerprints and DNA were on that gun; finally, it was accepted that the only DNA belonged to another person, who was later prosecuted and imprisoned in relation to it.

When preparing for the coroner's inquest, our team also had to deal with "closed material," which is intelligence material we were not allowed to see. The material could only be seen by a judge with clearance, following which the material was redacted and summarized before it could be presented to the court. What became clear to us was the degree of intelligence behind the shooting, both in respect to Mark and to others in Tottenham. Demonizing Mark served the purpose of deflecting attention from the details of this surveillance operation and from those who were under surveillance. In pursuit of this, Mark had to be characterized as the baddest man in Tottenham, the biggest gangster, all of that kind of stuff. You just have to look at the press coverage of the time. Usually when there's an encounter with a Black man, you hear that they're the strongest, most violent, most aggressive. They couldn't say that about Mark because he didn't have an opportunity to be aggressive. And so he was demonized in other ways.

That became a central theme in the inquest to justify his shooting. The jury finding raised complex concerns for the family in that their verdict was that Mark didn't have the gun in his hand but that he was "lawfully killed." The explanation that the police were in effect arguing self-defense has been understandably difficult for the family to comprehend, as opposed to the view that this was more in line with the practice of "shoot-to-kill." The family finds it interesting that the new police watchdog, the Independent Office for Police Conduct (IOPC), has said in response to the Forensic Architecture investigation that they are considering whether or not to reopen the investigation. We can but wait to see.

Mark's shooting was part of an operation known as Operation Dibri. The question this raises is whether this operation was concluded with the shooting in Tottenham, or whether this was part of a wider and continuing operation.

Najafi: Eyal, the police often justify such killings by claiming that they thought, in that split second in which they had to act, that their life was in danger. What is logic of the split second when used this way?

Weizman: The legal formulation of the "split second" connects two points, one made by Stafford — about "sus laws" and the Matrix — and other by Marcia about police manipulation of the notion of self-defense. They both expose the racist dimension of preemption — the state use of force, sometimes lethal, to "respond" not to something that has happened but to what they believe could happen or is about to happen. The landscape of risk that preemption opens depends to a large extent on racist perceptions in relation to inherent violence. So "sus laws" allowed the police to stop people for looking suspicious, for purported fear that they may do something, and the Matrix purportedly allows the police to preempt gang crime. Just like the "split second" argument, these are part of the entire scaffold of the logic of policing regarding what constitutes order and what qualifies as disorder. The order here refers to the order of white supremacy, which needs to be protected from people and actions that could pose a challenge to it.

The social order has to scan for risks before they emerge, and thus preemption is the place where systemic, societal racism is most clearly manifested. Racialized people are often believed to embody repressed violence that might explode at any moment.

This logic of preemption has, of course, colonial corollaries. Back where I come from, Palestinians simply walking through Jewish-majority cities — just like a Black person walking through a majority-white suburb — are seen as "ticking bombs," an attack about to happen, and they therefore should be stopped even if they have done nothing. Another related example is targeted assassinations from drones in Pakistan and Yemen, which are likewise articulated as preemptive action, with CIA predator drone operators justifying lethal action as responses to signs of an imminent attack. In the case of "signature drone strikes," this logic of preemption — like that of the Matrix, which Stafford has done a lot of work to oppose — is performed by algorithmic calculations. The preemption that drone murders and assassinations perform is justified by the legal category of "imminence," or imminent risk they pose — indeed, a "ticking bomb" that needs to be diffused. So imminence, in this type of manhunting that takes place in Waziristan or Gaza, is equivalent to the "split second" idea in cities. Over time, and with much abuse, what counts as imminent has become increasingly elastic, stretching and twisting the sense of temporal immediacy. Imminent cases can go on ticking for an awfully long time, to the degree that imminent risk becomes simply a political category. As an aside: the assassination of Iranian general Qassem Soleimani in January 2020 notionally relied on this definition, to the point where imminence lost all meaning.

So one of the questions for us is: how can we open up and extend the duration of imminence and the "split second" in order to connect it to longer history? In fact, Forensic Architecture was approached to help with this case after Richard Hammer, one of the barristers representing the family, saw a presentation of ours titled "The Long Duration of a Split Second," where we showed two cases we had undertaken involving police killings. One was in Palestine and the other concerned the shooting of a Black man in Chicago, and both were justified by the police as split-second decisions. In these cases, we unpacked the milliseconds of the incident, but also showed how learned cultural and systemic racism, nourished from a long history of settler-colonialism — and in the Duggan case, as Adam outlined, from imperial and colonial relations coming home — are condensed into the smallest possible fragment of time. In the case of the south Chicago police killing of Harith Augustus, who was just out on an errand, we narrated the incident across six timescales — milliseconds, seconds, minutes, hours, days, and years — to show how each bore on the incident in a different way.

Usually, we would undertake such analysis on the basis of videography. As Temi was saying, the police body cam, when it exists, distorts the perspective that viewers have onto an incident. They're pointed the wrong way; they're not really monitoring police action, but are aimed at the person the police are interacting with. In that, they are again criminalizing the person the police officer is looking at. When cases of police brutality are litigated, the body cams could generate something that is called "perspectival bias." Juries in the US seeing the situation from the perspective of a police officer tend to identify with the officer as a protagonist. Everybody who has seen this kind of footage knows that it is reminiscent of first-person shooter computer games. There's also the issue of the lens. Police cameras lenses are very wide-angle. When analyzing movement captured on body cams in relation to the same movement captured by a smart phone from further away, we noticed an interesting phenomenon. The wide-angle lens will make any movement — say, a hand movement — appear augmented or amplified, and so for those viewing the footage later, it can often seem more menacing than it actually was. This is just to say the obvious: no evidence, whether testimony or video, is perfectly faithful and neutral, and each is skewed in some way. The problem is that all evidence tends to be skewed toward the police.

Elliott-Cooper: The "split second" argument got me thinking about two things. I think it's something that the state and the media try to do a lot, which is to decontextualize or dehistoricize certain problems or issues. Nothing can decontextualize something more than offering only one thing to think about — the split second in which an officer makes a decision to kill Duggan instead of the hour up until that point where they decided to pursue him, or the months leading up to it when they were planning the operation.

In the inquest, when the lead police officer was being cross-examined, he was asked what lessons were learned from the operation. And he said that everything had gone as planned. They had already deemed themselves judge, jury, and executioner for Duggan, and they explicitly articulated this in court and received zero criticism for it. So the idea of "Let's just think about that split second and forget everything else" does the important work of decontextualizing. It's also helpful for the police because it creates the impression that racism is some kind of disease deep in the unconscious of some police officers that requires surgical removal, so that you can have this perfect, racism-free police officer once they've completed their unconscious bias training. The police love unconscious bias training.

I've been reading through the Metropolitan Police's equality and diversity agenda for 2021, and unconscious bias training is at the core of it because it's a really great training — they've got the funding for it, they can all go through it, and then they've been purged of the disease of racism forever and ever, which for some unknown reason was just deep in their unconscious and required removing. It serves this dual purpose of decontextualizing racism, but also treating it as a disease rather than as a power that has a really specific and important function in our society.

Mwale: I think the case of Azelle Rodney and the police marksman Anthony Long is really integral to this point. It's one that makes me deeply sick to my stomach. If you type in "Anthony Long," you'll find that his bosses joked that he was the Metropolitan Police's very own serial killer. He killed multiple people. And he was only ever charged with Azelle's murder. When you research him, you'll see, "the incredible career of the most controversial police marksman." His career has literally been shooting and killing predominantly Black people but this is something that can be lauded as "incredible" by the mainstream press.

I also read an article about how Long kept a file on all the dodgy, illegal things that his supervisors were doing. For him, his insurance policy was to not report anything his supervisors were doing. We're told that there are bad apples; surely, if there are these bad apples, then the rest of them are good apples and they would be reporting the illegal things that happen behind closed doors. The reality is that we have a rotten tree. We have police officers who carry weapons who have to have files on their bosses' unlawful things as insurance policies, so that in case they ever shoot and kill someone like Azelle Rodney, they will be able to say, "I'm on your side. You don't want to write me up for anything because I've got this file on you."

The reason I found it so disturbing is because this was all in mainstream newspapers. He admitted to this during the trial. It makes me question the kind of character we're building up in these officers, who rarely even face trial. It's not as if we can hold these people up and say, "It was just a split-second decision." The guy shot eight times; Azelle was hit six times, including several shots in the head. We can hear a voice recording of an officer saying "sweet" after every single shot. Even when we get a case to be heard, the jury, after hearing all of that evidence, still decides that it's better to uphold the fidelity of policing rather than admit that Long had done something illegal. And I'm deeply disturbed that he now works in private security, where he presents himself as this man who got away with it.

Scott: We also have to remember that prosecutors fail to properly prosecute police officers when they're charged. In the case of Duggan, this is the difficulty that we're facing with the decision that is being made now; the IOPC, who we're now asking to reverse the IPCC's decision, were part of the management team that took the original decision that every time they contracted an expert, the expert had to look at the scene and always imagine the gun being in Mark's hand. That totally biased the entire process, because it meant that they didn't at any time consider that the police planted it, even though there were IPCC notes where one of their investigators says that the police officers said that another officer placed the gun over there. It didn't get investigated at any time. That means that it was never put in front of a jury to consider at all.

Then finally, there's this bullshit notion of a police officer being able to say, "I had an honestly held belief." Ultimately, that is the safety net: "No matter how crazy everything I've said may sound, no matter what you find out there, I honestly believed that this person was a dangerous threat to me. So I did what I had to do." And how do you undermine the "honestly held belief" argument, especially when it's backed up with the notion that "I made a decision in that second"?

Elliott-Cooper: I think that this idea of honesty is really important. That's also where race and class come into it, with the fundamental presumption of honesty on the part of the state and the fundamental presumption of criminality and violence on the part of this young Black man. Unless you hold those two presumptions in your mind the whole time, none of it makes sense.

Najafi: Marcia, can you talk a bit more about the sequence of legal options in the Duggan case and how each one was blocked?

Willis Stewart: There was an inquest, which was mandatory as this was a death involving agents of the state. Alongside this, there were a number of complaints which were investigated by the IPCC, including complaints about the failure to inform the family, failure in respect to the gun — which had been involved in a previous incident that had nothing to do with Mark. With the investigation into the failure to contact the family, we actually had a positive outcome in that the police accepted that they had not done what they should have done. There was a change of protocol in terms of what's known as the death notice and the way the police are obliged to provide it to the family and next of kin. The investigation into the gun resulted in an individual being prosecuted and convicted. Also, the two officers involved in investigating the gun faced disciplinary proceedings for their failure to secure the gun long before it resurfaced in the Duggan shooting. The senior officer was disciplined for misconduct and the junior officer was fired. There were also civil proceedings, which were concluded in December 2019.

Najafi: How common is it for UK police to settle out of court?

Willis Stewart: This is now common following reforms in 1999. There is a risk of going to trial, for both the claimant and the defendant. Whilst the claimants who are funded by legal aid have to consider the risk of having funding removed if the merits of the claim change and/or a "reasonable offer" is made by the defendant, there is no doubt that the risk to the defendant in losing this claim would have been significant and would have had major ramifications for the Metropolitan Police and those officers involved in the shooting.

Najafi: Stafford, can you explain what the UK police's Matrix system is?

Scott: The Gangs Violence Matrix is a database that was created following the 2011 Duggan riots. Once the riots finished, David Cameron and Boris Johnson, the leader of the government and the mayor of London at the time, decided that the riots were the responsibility of gangs, even though they set up a number of different inquiries that told them differently, including the Metropolitan Police Service's own audit. They set up a lot of cross-party, cross-government initiatives and created bills that for the first time ever in UK legislation defined what constitutes a gang. In the UK, three people constitute a gang. Can you imagine that? Three people! I don't know what they would call those supergangs in the US. So they redefined the law and created this database called the Matrix in every borough to list all the individuals who they claim are gang members there.

At some point, I got a printed copy of the Matrix as it stood in 2016 for the borough of Haringey, where Tottenham is situated, and all but one of the people in it happened to be Black. Until very recently, the pan-London Matrix had around 3,800 people in it, and around three-quarters happened to be Black. In Haringey, the biggest gang is the Tottenham Boys, also known as the Tottenham Turks, a really organized, sophisticated gang, but the police are focusing on these little kids. Once you're in the database, which is algorithm-driven, you're given a "harm score" for how dangerous you might be, as well as a score for whether or not you've been a victim of gang crime. And even if the police don't think you are a gang member, they can add you to the list if you've been a victim of gang-related crime because they claim that that means that you might become involved in gang crime later, i.e., to seek violent revenge.

I wrote about the Matrix in January 2019 and Tottenham Rights made the Haringey database public at an April 2019 meeting in Tottenham where it was discussed with the community for the first time. The police subsequently had to take over a thousand names off the London database, and as a result of what we did, Amnesty International put in a complaint to the Information Commissioner's Office (ICO) about the nature of the database. The ICO carried out an investigation and found that in setting up the database, the police had broken all sorts of privacy, data, and equality legislation. And it was not just the police; it was the mayor of London and the Home Office. And they share that information right across the system — with the benefit office, the local authorities, housing, social services, and education, to the extent that it is the end of these young people's lives once they're in the database. It kills people. And it causes so much frustration amongst the young people who are caught up in it that this is what is really fueling the violence that you see happening in London today.

Najafi: Temi, could you tell us about the work that your organization does?

Mwale: I set up the 4Front Project in 2012 after my childhood friend was murdered. I wanted to provide a platform for young people who have been impacted by serious violence to create change in society. Policing and the criminal justice system claim to keep us safe and address the harm that results from violence, but that is not the effect they have. Through a range of services, including mentoring, advocacy, youth activism training, creative support, and more, 4Front supports some of the young people most directly harmed — not just by violence in the community, but by policing and the criminal justice system itself. Our work centers healing and transformative justice whilst directly challenging the UK's addiction to criminalization, policing, and prisons.

I think the most important thing to say at this stage is that policing doesn't work. The deaths in police custody are really at one extreme and I'm pleased that they're being investigated and gaining the exposure that they deserve. But that's the tip of the iceberg; the culture of violence that enables those deaths, like Duggan's and others' that we've discussed today, has so many victims. 4Front supports many of those young people who are victims of everyday brutality, abuse, and harassment. I originally got involved in the Justice for Mark Duggan campaign because I had already set up 4Front at that time and I was working with young people who were being labeled by professionals from the outside world as "gang members." What the murder of Mark Duggan showed me was that anybody who can be labeled in this way can be executed on the street, even in broad daylight. Not only will nobody care, the media will have a field day.

I want to share something that's always stayed with me. I was only fifteen when Duggan was killed, so I didn't really know much about the activism around deaths in custody. I was young and naive, but I did know about police harassment and brutality in the everyday sense because, well, which young people growing up in communities like mine don't know about that? I was at school doing my A levels and studying law, and we had a class on law and morality. And when I talked about Mark Duggan, my law teacher said that he was a gangster, so it was actually good that he got killed — basically he deserved it. Bear in mind, he's supposed to be teaching us what the law actually is. He didn't tell us anything about the fact that there's legislation and mandatory minimum sentencing related to the possession and use of firearms. In fact, he didn't tell us about the law at all in terms of how it related to this case. He inserted his opinion, which was based on what was being said in the media and by the police: that because he was a "gang member," it was basically okay for him to be killed by the police in the way that he was.

That was a significant moment for me, because I realized that this was a type of oppression I was facing in school. There's such a disconnect here; we've seen over the last couple of months with the reinvigoration of the Black Lives Matter movement, especially in this country, that it's so easy to point the finger abroad. People want to talk about George Floyd and Breonna Taylor, though they wouldn't be able to point to Minneapolis or Louisville on a map. I'm okay with that because international solidarity is fundamental, but the British public has almost no idea of the scale of abuse within policing, the scale of deaths in custody, happening on their very own doorstep. And there is very little will, or maybe desire, to interrogate it because it would force you to understand the colonial legacy that Adam's talking about.

I feel so inspired and motivated by the work that happened in the 1980s that Stafford described. I met Stafford through the Justice for Mark Duggan campaign, and I didn't know much about the history of Broadwater Farm or its youth association and all the activism that young people were being empowered to do. And I think it's interesting that decades later, we have 4Front, which is doing something very similar to what the Broadwater Farm Youth Association was doing in the 1980s: that is, understanding that in our community there are young people who are being targeted, harassed, and criminalized by an oppressive force, so that it essentially feels like our community, Grahame Park estate, is being occupied. Stafford said that they made sure there was no police station on Broadwater Farm, but we're right next to Colindale police station, and right next to Hendon, the training center for all police. And we also have a police center on the estate, where there have been many reports of young people being unlawfully strip-searched and abused.

We're talking about young people who have been ostracized and marginalized — excluded from school at such rates that we can't even fully articulate the impact; discriminated against in terms of housing, educational opportunities, and employment; having to live in impoverished areas; exposed to extreme harm, trauma, and violence — but it's the police who have been put in place to manage them. And by "manage them," I mean that they're seen as a burden to society. They're not seen as part of the community because when the police try to justify their treatment, they say, "Well, the community is calling us and saying they don't like young people hanging out outside or smoking cannabis." And it's like, "Why are the young people that you're harassing not seen as part of the community?" So, part of our work is to transform that narrative. These young people are just as much a part of this community as anyone else. And actually, part of the community does not want the policing we see here, does not want a police center on the estate, because the experience of our section of the community is extremely different from people who are even living next door.

That's part of the issue: that even someone living next door can have completely different experiences, completely different views on history and of policing. What happens when you mobilize young people by helping them understand the historical context for what's happening to them and what happened to generations before them, and that their resistance to it is part of an evolving struggle that didn't just come from nowhere? What happens when you mobilize young people to advocate for their own rights, for their communities and families? They know it's not right, but they feel so subdued by the scale of harassment that sometimes they don't want to make complaints, not only because it is emotionally draining, but because they have no faith that anything will be addressed.

If Mark Duggan can be killed, if they can be abused every single day with no repercussions, why would they complain? But the fact that there are very few complaints is taken as evidence that there are very few issues, rather than a lack of confidence in the system of accountability for policing. We're trying to create space for young people to envision how they can build a new system of accountability. How can we work with the young people who are most harmed by criminal justice? Because it's not just policing; we're working with young people who are being put on a conveyor belt into prison, with young people who have experienced criminal justice because of the way our communities are being treated. How can we try to build new systems for healing and accountability that not only look at the harm that's been caused by the state, but the harm that we're causing to each other within the communities, which is used in turn to justify the current systems of policing and criminal justice?

I see that work as deeply connected to the kind of work that has taken place across the world in many other places that are trying to interrogate these systems. It's a cycle of pain and harm and trauma. And that is the fundamental disconnect, because nobody is willing to admit that the police and criminal justice system inflict trauma, and there are no services to deal with that. We've had mayor's offices across the country over the last couple of years say, "Let's have a public health approach to violence." And Cressida Dick says that with her as the commissioner, the Metropolitan Police are implementing a public health approach to violence. Apparently, they are "trauma-informed." I laugh. How can the police, who have the sole monopoly on legally justifiable violence and domination, even when they act unlawfully, be trauma-informed?

What we've just started to unpack with the Gang Matrix database is how professionals from all these different institutions — the local authorities, schools, and even hospitals and mental health services — actually get together through multi-agency meetings and prop up the criminal justice system. Take police intelligence, for example. We have local councils using so-called police "intelligence" on one young person who's potentially in the Matrix database to try and evict the whole family. We have the job centers run by the Department for Work and Pensions, where people are supposed to get support for seeking a job; they have more gang members listed in their own database than the Metropolitan Police themselves. I don't know how the workers in the job center are in a position to identify who's in a so-called gang and who's not. The reality is that we can't just be speaking about the harm of policing without looking at how all these other public agencies and the state in all its other forms intertwine with the police and the criminal justice system and further the harm and abuse. □

## WITNESS STATEMENT

CJ Act 1967, s.9 MC Act 1980, ss 5A(3)(a) and 5B; MC Rules 1981, r70

Statement of  *Q63*

Age if under 18  (if over 18 inset 'over 18')

Occupation  *Police Officer*

This statement (consisting of  page(s) each signed by me) is true to the best of my knowledge and belief and I make it knowing that, if it is tendered in evidence, I shall be liable to prosecution if I have wilfully stated in it anything which I know to be false or do not believe to be true.

Date: *4th August 2011*  Time: *2300.*

Signature:  *Q63.*

*On Thursday 4th August 2011 I was on duty in plain clothes in company with other plain clothed officers. I was the driver of a covert armed response vehicle ( ▇▇▇ ) Va Grey BMW Saloon. I was in possession of my personal issue Glock 17 SP, issue number 184 which was holstered and my MP5 Carbine, reg number T21. This was loaded and made ready and was secured in the boot of our vehicle. I do had a taser (x08). In my vehicle, R31 was operating and W39 was in the rear on maps. We were on duty c*

Signature:_____

*Above: The first page of Q63's account of the Duggan shooting in his Evidence and Action Book. The account continues on page 47 at lower left. This and all other images through page 61 are from the National Archives.*

Documents

Our investigation sought to account for the critical question at the heart of the case: How did the gun get to the grass?

There are three main routes: either Duggan threw the gun during the encounter with the police officers after he had stepped out of the minicab, as the IPCC concluded; he threw the gun as he was exiting the minicab, as the coroner's inquest jury thought was most likely; or the police officers moved it to where they said it was found.

Our work began with thousands of pages of documents: witness statements, sworn testimony, expert reports, plans, diagrams, and maps. Each of the thirteen officers involved wrote detailed statements, which were then used by the IPCC, and all but one were subsequently interviewed before a judge at the coroner's inquest.[1] We combed through these documents and cross-referenced them, gaining an understanding of the events that led to Duggan's killing through a necessarily compromised lens: the partial, overlapping, and at times contradictory accounts of the officers.

The following pages present a selection of these documents. We begin with pages from the officers' handwritten logbooks (known as Evidence and Action Books, or EABs), in which, on the evening of 4 August 2011, most of them wrote their initial assessments of the events of earlier that day. These assessments are cursory but can nonetheless be extremely revealing in what details they include, or omit.

These are followed by an excerpt of the transcript of the coroner's inquest from 15 October 2013, the day on which various lawyers questioned V53, the officer who shot and killed Duggan. At the inquest, officers were interviewed about the content of their detailed statements — the majority of which were written three days after the incident — and of their EABs, and asked to clarify and disentangle their written claims. However, a coroner's inquest is *inquisitorial* rather than *adversarial*, meaning that the lawyers involved are unable to strongly challenge the accounts they hear. At times, this frustration is evident in the lawyers' tone.

Some documents we examined cannot be presented here, as they have not been released into the public domain. The officers' detailed statements, for example, remain classified by the Metropolitan Police, though much of their content was discussed in public at the inquest.[2] The majority of those statements, as well as the EAB reports, were produced in circumstances that lawyers for the Duggan family protested both during and after the inquest. On both 4 and 7 August, officers gathered, unsupervised, to write their accounts: on the evening of the shooting, ten of the thirteen officers wrote their initial EAB reports together at their headquarters in Leman Street, east London; three days later, eleven of them wrote their detailed statements together at the same location. This left open the possibility of their conferring and agreeing upon key aspects of their accounts.[3]

Going through these documents, we looked for passages in which officers described the spatial layout of the scene and made claims about where they and others stood, and about what they saw or missed at any given moment. This was our way of examining whether what they presented as their "honestly held belief" agreed with the objective facts. In the process, we identified and recorded two other types of irregularity that challenged the very possibility of "honest belief," which forms the legal basis for how the police defend themselves after such shootings: instances where a description by one officer contradicted those of others, and instances where a similarly worded, but demonstrably false, description occurred throughout, suggesting that the officers might have coordinated their accounts.

1. Officer V72, the driver for the so-called control vehicle — the car that took up a position behind the other three during the hard top — was the only officer not interviewed in person at the inquest. His statement was read into the public record on 3 December 2013. None of the four officers in the control car left their vehicle until after the shooting.

2. The EAB reports of seven of the nine officers in the front three cars were made public through the coroner's inquest. Those written by V53 and R31 were not.

3. The three who were not present on 4 August were the two senior officers, ZZ17 and Z51, as well as V53, who received legal advice after the incident and was interviewed by representatives from the IPCC, the police officers' union, and the Metropolitan Police's Directorate of Professional Standards. On 7 August, ZZ17 and Z51 were again not present, though V53 joined his colleagues to write his detailed statement. The absent officers did write EAB reports and detailed statements, albeit separately.

## NOTES OF ARREST/REPORT OF INCIDENT

| | |
|---|---|
| TIME NOTES STARTED: | 2258 |
| TIME NOTES COMPLETED: | 2355 |
| LOCATION NOTES MADE: | HD |
| PERSONS PRESENT. | V48, R68, W70, W56 |
| | W39, R31, V72, V59, Q63, W42 |

It is essential that you record a complete account of events. It is intended to protect you from needless civil action or complaint investigation. You MUST follow the following guidance. Your notes will be subject to close scrutiny. You may confer with other officers who were present for an overview, but these notes are to assist YOUR recollection.

**Background**

- Set the scene: As fully as possible "on day, date, time, place, etc."
- State the information you had before attending the scene, this will help explain your actions.
- If notes were not made at scene, explain fully.
- Do not mention sensitive sources/techniques.

**Action**

- State what happened when you arrived.
- Record all questions asked/answers given both before and after caution. **Keep an open mind.** You are duty bound to gather all evidence and entitled to question any person from whom useful information can be obtained. **You should include hearsay.**
- Fully record your actions and the options considered **up to the point of arrest.**
- Show what factors influenced your decision, include reasons for *not* taking action.

continued on next page

*Excerpts from the Evidence and Action Books of three of the ten officers who produced their first statements together on the night of the shooting, 4 August 2011: W70 (this page), W42 (opposite, top row), and Q63 (opposite, bottom left).*

Other Ref. No.

---

## WITNESS STATEMENT
CJ Act 1967, s.9 MC Act 1980, ss 5A(3)(a) and 5B; MC Rules 1981, r70

Statement of **R W70**

Age if under 18 over 18 (if over 18 inset 'over 18')

Occupation **Police officer.**

This statement (consisting of **2** page(s) each signed by me) is true to the best of my knowledge and belief and I make it knowing that, if it is tendered in evidence, I shall be liable to prosecution if I have wilfully stated in it anything which I know to be false or do not believe to be true.

Date: **4/8/11**      Time: **2355**

Signature: **W70**

ON THURSDAY 4th AUGUST 2011 I was on duty in plain clothes as an authorised firearms officer attached to ▓▓▓ C019. We paraded at 1600 hrs at LEMAN ST POLICE STATION I was posted as rear seat passenger in ▓▓▓▓ in comply with R68 who was driving and V53 who was front seat passenger. I was deployed with my personal issue Glock 17 SLP (number ▓▓▓)

Signature: **W70.**

Other Ref. No.

---

Continued: personal issue MPS ▓ both in condition 1 and HATTON GUN (▓). At approximate 1813 hrs we were tasked to stop a vehicle index R343 kPE as part of an going operation That stop took place on FERRY LANE N17 close to TOTTENHAM HALE STATION. I deployed from the vehicle and during the course of this stop a number of rounds were discharged and as a result 1 subject was hit and 1 police officer. 1st AID was given to both parties by police. I remained at scene until returning to LEMAN ST POLICE STATION to take part in PIP procedure. W70 ▓▓▓▓▓▓ W70

Signature: **W70**

## WITNESS STATEMENT

CJ Act 1967, s.9 MC Act 1980, ss 5A(3)(a) and 5B; MC Rules 1981, r70

Statement of  W42.

Age if under 18         (if over 18 inset 'over 18')

Occupation

This statement (consisting of      page(s) each signed by me) is true to the best of my knowledge and belief and I make it knowing that, if it is tendered in evidence, I shall be liable to prosecution if I have wilfully stated in it anything which I know to be false or do not believe to be true.

Date: 4TH of AUGUST 2011      Time: 00:00

Signature: W42.                (05-08-11)

ON THURSDAY 4TH of AUGUST 2011, I WAS ON DUTY IN PLAIN CLOTHES ASSIGNED AS 2ic (2ND IN CHARGE) of TROJAN ▓▓▓▓▓▓▓▓▓▓▓▓▓▓▓▓. ON THIS DAY, I WAS TASKED WITH STOPPING A PEOPLE CARRIER MOTOR VEHICLE REG R343 KPE, THE OCCUPANT of WHICH WAS BELIEVED TO BE IN POSSESSION of A GUN.

I WAS ARMED WITH MY PERSONAL

Signature: W42.

---

Continued: ISSUE GLOCK 17 SLP, WHICH WAS CARRIED & HOLSTERED & MY PERSONAL ISSUE MP5 (BOTT ▓▓) WHICH WAS IN CONDITION ONE. THE VEHICLE WAS STOPPED IN FERRY LANE, N17

I WAS SUDDENLY AWARE OF SHOTS BEING FIRED, ONE of WHICH HIT ME ON MY left SIDE — I WAS IMMEDIATELY TAKEN to THE GROUND & TAKEN TO BY MY COLLEAGUES.

I WAS TAKEN TO HOSPITAL, WITH NO INJURIES AS THE BULLET H/O STRUCK MY RADIO

W42

Signature: W42

---

Continued: HOUSE. At about 1800HRS I/C was asked to carry out a stop on a people carrier, index R343KPE as it was believed that the occupant of the vehicle was in possession of a firearm. I/C located the vehicle in FERRY LANE and at about 1815HRS a non-compliant stop was implemented. As I ran towards the rear of the vehicle, I heard ~~bangs~~ a number of shots being fired as I saw a black male fall to the floor. A police officer had also been shot. I co-ordinated other resources whilst first aid was given. I videoed 1'' AID of the black male until life was pronounced ▓▓▓ after I left the scene.

Signature: Q63

---

V53's EAB has never been made public. No explanation has been given for this decision.

*This and following five pages: Excerpt from V53's questioning at the coroner's inquest, 15 October 2013, containing his description of the incident from the time the minicab was brought to a stop to the moment when the officer loses sight of the gun that he claims was in Duggan's hand. The testimony also provides insight into V53's impression of his own perception, as he breaks up the scene into "split seconds" and "freeze-frames."*

1  Q.  What was your thought process about the minicab driver?

2  A.  Again, the minicab driver -- again, we've experience of

3      dealing with minicab drivers in this kind of scenario.

4      Again, it's a bit of a MO for gangs within London to use

5      minicabs because it does not draw attention to them, if

6      they're driving around in a minicab in the back.

7      So, again, the majority of the time the minicab

8      driver will be an innocent member of the public.

9      However, there may be some occasions where they may be

10     told, you know, here is £10, forget what you've seen and

11     bits and pieces.  So, again, we didn't have any

12     intelligence actually on the minicab driver but we would

13     treat him as an unknown risk.

14  Q.  Just on this, if what I call a "hard stop" is called

15     a "non-compliance stop" in police terms, was there any

16     reason to believe the minicab would be non-compliant?

17  A.  We didn't have any intelligence, sir, no.

18  Q.  Do you know whether any thought was put to some other

19     form of stopping the minicab if the driver might have

20     been innocent?

21  A.  No.  Again, the threat is the person in the rear

22     because, again, the taxi driver could be -- or in this

23     particular case was -- a innocent member of the public.

24     If we had done perhaps a different tactic, there may be

25     a chance that the subject in the rear of the cab may

34

1     actually hold the driver hostage or hold him under

2     duress.  So, again, by doing the tactic of

3     a non-compliant hard stop, we're trying to prevent the

4     subject from escaping, from doing any violence, but,

5     again, the main thing is we are trying to maximum the

6     safety of the public by isolating him from the public.

7     So there's the subject, armed police and members of

8     the public, so we're trying to isolate the subject from

9     members of the public, so we're actually trying to

10    maximise the safety of the minicab driver by doing

11    a hard stop.

12  Q.  Right.  Did there come a point where you were listening

13    to commentary over the radio of the surveillance team

14    following the minicab?

15  A.  Yes, we did, sir, yes.

16  Q.  How was that described, that minicab?

17  A.  The minicab to me was an old style gold people carrier

18    the registration number was R343 KPE.

19  Q.  Let's have a look at this since we're on your statement

20    at page 75, the top paragraph.  You say:

21    "I heard commentary that the target vehicle/minicab

22    which was an old style gold people carrier [you give the

23    registration] was in Blackhorse Road in front of a BMW

24    X5.  I scanned the road in front of me, saw the X5 and

25    in front of it I clearly identified the minicab.  It's

35

distinctive due to its 'gold' like colour and mirror in
its back window."

Q. Officer, it was silver, wasn't it?

A. I don't know, sir. I would probably describe it as
gold, to be honest with you, I recall.

Q. Let's take this in stages. First of all we know from
ZZ37 that he described it as bronze; do you recall that?

A. No, sir, I don't.

Q. The commentary may well have had "bronze" in it; do you
recall?

A. I don't recall, sir, no.

Q. "Gold" is used twice in the flip charts that V59 put
together for the briefing on 7 August; do you recall
that?

A. I do, sir, yes.

Q. Everybody seems to describe it either as bronze from
that commentary or gold from the flip charts. I'll be
corrected if I'm wrong by saying it's everybody but at
least a large number of the officers making notes and
making their statements on 7 August pick up that colour
scheme.

A. Okay, sir.

Q. Now, you're saying, are you, that you remember it as
being gold?

A. That's how I would describe it, sir, yes. It was

36

distinctive because of its gold colour and particularly
the mirror that was on the back window of it.

Q. If I were to suggest to you the possibility that you've
written down on 7 August the word "gold" simply because
it was put on the flip charts, that would be wrong,
would it?

A. That would be wrong, sir, yes.

Q. Let's move on. We've got you now in convoy following
the minicab, you've caught sight of it and there's a BMW
X5 between it and police vehicles. What happened then?
Again, as best you can recall, please.

A. Yes. We're in Ferry Lane, so we're undertaking traffic
so we're trying to be covert as possible, because if we
start overtaking vehicles on the wrong side of the road
and bits and pieces, somebody who's surveillance-aware
is going to clock us and they're going to be on their
toes even quicker. So again, we're trying to be as
covert as possible but at the same time we're trying to
make progress as naturally as possible through the
traffic. Again we're in plain clothes and in plain
clothes cars.

We got behind the X5 and then beyond the X5 was the
minicab, and then the minicab -- not the minicab -- the
X5, pulled -- turned left, I don't know the road name,
but that basically left the Alpha, Bravo, Charlie and

37

our control car directly behind the minicab.

Q. What happened then?

A. Once we got there, state red was called, I remember, and
then W42, who's in the lead vehicle, he called "Strike,
strike, strike".

Q. Did you see the stop go in?

A. Yes, I did, yes. Again, we were reaching the brow of
the bridge of Ferry Lane, so you've got a large grassed
area round to the left, you've got a pillar and then
you've got, like, a five/six foot fence line to the
nearside and a footpath. The minicab is going and then
the Alpha car overtakes and then (indicates) the Bravo
car overtakes and my car, the Charlie car, we stay at
the back.

The Alpha car -- basically, what we're trying to do
is enforce that vehicle to stop, that minicab is going
to stop whether it wants to or not because we need to
stop that vehicle. So, again, the Alpha car cuts in in
front, at an angle (indicates). the Bravo car goes
alongside and then the vehicle I'm in, the Charlie car,
we go up the back of the minicab leaving around a couple
of inch gap.

So where we actually stop is directly behind the
minicab, as close as possible, to prevent that minicab
from ramming his way out or trying to escape by

38

vehicular access (indicates).

Q. Did that go to plan?

A. It did, yes indeed. Initially, the minicab, I would
say, didn't stop as quickly as we would have liked, it
wasn't failing the stop or anything. Again, normally we
would not necessarily use two tones but I remember two
tones being used or "whoop woo", for a better word,
being used to bring the car to a halt.

Q. Was there any delay in any one of the cars getting into
position?

A. No, not that I recall.

Q. Can we look at page CE263. It will come up on your
screen, I hope, even if not all the others. Is this
a plan you drew, do you recall?

A. Yes, I've signed that. That was given to the IPCC at
some stage.

Q. The Alpha car is not on here because it had been moved
by the time the laser scan took place.

A. Indeed.

Q. The BMW directly behind the minicab is your car, isn't
it?

A. It is indeed, sir, yes.

Q. As far as you're concerned, is that where it did indeed
stop?

A. It did indeed, yes. It wasn't moved.

39

Q. Keeping that in front of us, we'll go back to your
statement if we have to but keeping that up, tell us
what happened next?

A. As the strike happened, (indicates) as we're slowing
down, Mark Duggan is sat behind the rear nearside of the
minicab, so he is sat behind the driver. As the stop
goes in, I'm looking towards and he then darts across
the back seat from right to left -- I would describe at
pace -- and that took, you know, my mindset at that time
was he's looking to escape because of his actions. So
again, as we put the hit in, he's darting across the
back seat of the minicab from right to left towards the
door.

Q. While the vehicles were still moving or after?

A. I think it was -- just came to a halt or there or
thereabouts.

Q. Then what happened?

A. At that time, I start to get out of my vehicle, at that
time I would have put a blue baseball cap on and, as I'm
in the process of opening my car door or there or
thereabouts, I saw W42, who came from the Alpha car. He
would have been the front seat passenger, he's armed
with a MP5 carbine, he has a police baseball cap on and
he is shouting into the structure of the minicab where
Mark Duggan still is, and he's shouting "Armed police".

40

Q. Whereabouts -- looking at the plan we've got on screen
you're just getting out of your car, are you?

A. Yes, I'm in the process of probably opening the door a
getting out.

Q. Still on the -- either in the car or on the road rathe
than the pavement?

A. Yes, I cannot be precise. I would have been in the
process of exiting that car, I believe.

Q. Where was W42?

A. I can't be precise. He would have been on the paveme
before -- obviously the sliding door, I cannot be
precise. He would have been on the footpath.

Q. By the side of the minicab, though?

A. Yes. He would have been aiming towards the minicab o
the structure of the minicab.

Q. So very close to where Mr Duggan would be coming out,
Mr Duggan came out?

A. Yes, I would probably say so, yes. Again, I cannot g
a distance but, yes, he would be very close.

Q. What did you see then?

A. As I start to get out as well, the minicab door opens
and Mark Duggan jumped out. The way I describe this
he's jumped out at pace, you know, he has a spring in
his step, and that again convinced me that he was
looking to escape.

41

Q. Let's just stop there, please. From the angle you would
have been at, if you were either by your car door or on
the pavement or the kerb there, could you see the door
itself slide or are you assuming that the door slid
open?

A. You can sort of see, because of the sliding -- the way
the door slides, you can see it's sort of going
parallel, if that makes sense. So if that's the door
(indicates), you can sort of see sliding back, if that
makes sense.

Q. So you were sufficiently on the pavement were you to be
able to see the minicab side?

A. I believe so, yes. I definitely seen the door slide
open.

THE ASSISTANT CORONER: You saw the door sliding open?

A. Yes. Along the rails on the side of the car.

THE ASSISTANT CORONER: The side of the minicab, yes.

MR UNDERWOOD: What did you see of Mr Duggan then? You saw
him coming out at a pace?

A. Yes, he's jumped out at pace and initially he's facing
towards W42, and then at that time I'm getting out of my
vehicle and I'm -- I take a couple of steps towards and
I've got my MP5 in the off-aim ready position.

Q. There's a box marked "A" there, what does that
represent?

42

A. That represents the area roughly where I would have b
standing.

Q. So, again, let's take a snapshot: W42, before the doo
slides, is close by that door, is he?

A. He would be -- can I point?

Q. Please.

A. Again, I cannot be precise, but he would have been
(indicates) somewhere along there, I believe.

THE ASSISTANT CORONER: Perhaps you can say where he's
pointing, I can't see.

MR UNDERWOOD: Somewhere around the front quarter of the
minicab, on the pavement.

A. Yes, sir, yes.

THE ASSISTANT CORONER: Are you pointing that he's gone
forward from the door that he got out of?

A. No, he would not be past the sliding door, but I thin
he was somewhere on the pavement, sort of near, maybe
the engine block of the minicab. Again, I cannot be
precise.

THE ASSISTANT CORONER: The engine being at the front of
minicab, so he's gone past where the word "mini" is,
then gone forward to the front of the minicab firstly

A. Yes, I think he's towards the front, so the engine bl
of the minicab, I believe, sort of within that rough
area. But again, sir, I cannot be precise exactly wh

43

he was.

THE ASSISTANT CORONER:  I understand.

MR UNDERWOOD:  You are somewhere around the box marked "A"
on that plan?

A.  Yes, sir, yes.

Q.  Mr Duggan is coming out with a spring in his step.
We've all got experience of that minicab or replica of
the minicab and how easy or difficult it is to get out.
The experience, I think, is that you pretty much have to
contort yourself to get out.

A.  Okay.

Q.  What was his stance?

A.  Again, he turned to face W42, I can't really say what
stance, he was sort of -- I think his knees were maybe
slightly bent so -- but I cannot really give you any
more than that because his back was towards me at that
time.

Q.  Then what happened?

A.  At that time, as I'm in an off-aim ready position,
I've -- W42 has shouted "Armed police" -- "Stand still,
stand still" and at the same time I've shouted "Armed
police".

Q.  What did Mr Duggan do?

A.  At that time he turned to face me.  I don't know if he
turned left or to his right but Mr Duggan has done like

44

1  a pivot movement and he's turned to face me.  So at that
2  time, if I could describe it, I'm in an off-aim
3  position, I've got lovely peripheral vision over the top
4  and I'm taking everything in.
5  Q.  Over the top of what?
6  A.  Over the sight.  The weapon is slightly down, so I'm
7  looking across everything so I'm trying to take
8  everything in.
9  Q.  Had he actually parted from the minicab or did he have
10  one foot on it or what?
11  A.  No he was out of the minicab.
12  Q.  How far out, do you think?
13  A.  I don't know, sir, not very far.
14  Q.  Okay.  Then what happened?
15  A.  The only way I can describe it is like a freeze frame
16  moment.  You know, it's like if you've got Sky Plus or
17  a video recorder, it's where you start pausing things,
18  and in my head the world had stopped because as he's
19  turned to face me, where I had lovely peripheral vision
20  my focus turned immediately to what was in his hand.
21  Q.  How was he holding his hand?
22  A.  Again, may I stand up?
23  THE ASSISTANT CORONER:  Yes, please, yes.
24  A.  As he's turned to face me, he has an object in his right
25  hand (indicates), Mark Duggan is carrying a handgun in

45

his right hand.  I can see the handle of the weapon,
I can make out the trigger guard, I can make out the
barrel and it's side-on to his body and there's a black
sock covering that weapon.

THE ASSISTANT CORONER:  Can you just turn round with your
hand in the position?

A.  Like this (indicates).

MR UNDERWOOD:  What you are describing is right arm close in
by the chest, elbow bent, right hand across your
chest -- across your stomach, really.

THE ASSISTANT CORONER:  Across your stomach, over your
navel, isn't it?

A.  It is.  Side-on to his stomach and the weapon is
parallel to the floor.

MR UNDERWOOD:  I don't know whether we have that gun in its
sock now?

THE ASSISTANT CORONER:  We'll come back to that, I think.

MR UNDERWOOD:  Perhaps you could have your Glock back -- not
your Glock, a Glock back.  (Handed)

A.  (Indicates)

Q.  So the gun was being held without the finger in the
trigger guard?

A.  I don't recall, I just remember he was holding it with
his right hand.  Again, you can make out the shape
outline of it, the handle of it, the barrel, you could

46

1  make out the trigger guard, not visually, but again if
2  you image it going as a L-shape, the sock, there's like
3  a little bit of give in it, so that's where the trigger
4  guard would have been, and obviously the size of the
5  object was similar size to my side arm.
6  MR UNDERWOOD:  Again, can I have that please because I am on
7  camera and you are not?
8  THE ASSISTANT CORONER:  Please.  I'll ask Mr Underwood just
9  to imitate that.  (Handed)
10  MR UNDERWOOD:  Thanks.  You're describing this, I think; is
11  that fair (indicates)?
12  A.  Slightly lower down, sir.  The barrel is more parallel
13  to the floor and the elbow is kind of more tucked in.
14  Q.  Like that?
15  A.  Yes.
16  Q.  (Indicates) So it's aiming left?
17  A.  It is, yes.
18  Q.  Despite the fact there's a sock on it, you think his
19  hand has gripped the grip rather than -- not doing that
20  (indicates)?
21  A.  No, he was holding that weapon.
22  Q.  But not like that, with his finger in the trigger?
23  A.  I do not remember where his top finger is, his trigger
24  finger was.
25  Q.  Thanks.  (Handed)

47

                Can you help us about what his stance was then?

A.  If I recall, his knees were slightly bent (indicates).
    He was not standing up straight and proud but he wasn't
    fully bent down as well, if that makes sense.

Q.  Okay, yes.  What about his relationship with you?  Was
    he square on to you or three-quarters on or sideways on
    or what?

A.  Again, I cannot be precise because, you know, this is
    happening in seconds but he was facing me, he may have
    been slightly to the left of me, but, again, I can't be
    100 per cent precise.

Q.  Broadly speaking, upright and, broadly speaking, square
    on to you; would that be fair?

A.  Yes, sir.

Q.  Moving?

A.  Again, the only way I can describe this moment is the
    world has just stopped in my head, it's like a freeze
    frame moment and, again, the only thing I was focused on
    was the gun.

Q.  Right.  What did you do?

A.  Again, because he was carrying it like this (indicates),
    again I've assessed and at that time he's not posing
    a threat to me.  So, again, I'm hoping he's going to
    drop it or he's going to do something.  Again, this is
    happening in milliseconds but then the next thing he

                                48

does, he starts to move the gun away from his body
(indicates).

Q.  The way you are describing that is that all you're
    moving is your wrist; is that right?

A.  Yes.

Q.  So he was not flinging his arm out --

A.  No.

Q.  -- or flexing his elbow?

A.  No, in this movement.  So he's moved the weapon, the
    barrel, he raised the weapon (indicates), moved it
    a couple of inches away from his body.

THE ASSISTANT CORONER:  Can you turn round a little bit
    I can see as well?

A.  Sorry, sir.

MR UNDERWOOD:  You used the word raised but it's not been
    raised up, it's being brought out.

A.  I would use the word "raised" because it describes
    a movement in my head.  So to me he's raised it.

THE ASSISTANT CORONER:  He's swinging it around, out from
    his body, but the hand still remains on his stomach.

MR UNDERWOOD:  He's, at that stage, still square on to you

A.  Yes, still square on.

Q.  What did you do then?

A.  Again because -- the only way I can describe this,
    there's a line in the sand now or there's a tipping

                                49

point.  If Mr Duggan had left the gun like this I would
have hoped he would have dropped it, but because he's
moved it away from his body I now have an honest held
belief he's going to shoot me, because by moving away
from his body he can do this (indicates) or he can do
this (indicates) in a fraction of a second, whereby
I had an honest held belief that he was going to shoot
me.

Q.  What you have just demonstrated there is that either he
    could raise his arm up, so it is parallel to the ground,
    and aim the gun at you and shoot you or he can just
    swing --

A.  He could swing it like this, sir, yes.

Q.  -- the gun further round and shoot you with his elbow
    still crooked against his chest, yes?

A.  Indeed, sir, yes.

Q.  What then did happen?

A.  Again -- because, again, the tipping point or the line
    in the sand -- because he's actually moved it away from
    his body, I have a honest held belief he's going to
    shoot me.  So I had my MP5 in an off-aim ready position
    and -- again this is happening in a split second.
        So again I brought my weapon up (indicates) and I've
    discharged one round and I'm aiming for the central body
    mass because I'm looking to shoot to stop, to achieve --

                                50

basically stop the threat.  So I've discharged one
round.

Q.  Did you see that impact on him?

A.  I did, sir, yes.

Q.  Then what happened?

A.  Again, if I may describe, sir.  (Indicates) the gun
    initially like this, the round has impacted Mr Duggan
    his right chest and it's caused like a flinching
    movement.

Q.  You have described there him flinching with his right
    shoulder away from you?

A.  If that's -- yes (indicates).

THE ASSISTANT CORONER:  Again, it's very important the jury
    see firstly, but it's also quite important that I see
    well.

A.  So, sir, as I say, he's moved the gun barrel away from
    his body a couple of inches I've discharged one round
    which has impacted on his chest, which has caused like
    a flinching movement, and then the gun has now moved
    is now pointing towards my direction.

THE ASSISTANT CORONER:  Flinching movement is the right
    shoulder going sharply back?

A.  It is, sir, yes, from the impact of the round.

THE ASSISTANT CORONER:  So whereabouts are you saying the
    round had impacted.

                                51

A. On his right chest.

MR UNDERWOOD: Again, can I have the gun back and I'll, with your guidance, do that so that it can be seen on the camera. (Indicates) so starting from down here somewhere (indicates), you see --

A. Yes, sir.

Q. -- a round go in around there.

A. Right chest, yes.

Q. He flinches that way away (indicates)?

A. Yes, but the gun has come out.

Q. So he has moved the gun out towards you before you fired, the round hits him up there?

A. Yes.

Q. He flinches away?

A. I wouldn't say he's flinched that much.

Q. He reacts away, right shoulder away from you and the gun is now trained more towards you.

A. It is indeed, sir, yes.

Q. (Handed)

Thanks very much. Then what happened?

A. Again, I've reassessed what's happening in front of me, so again -- this is happening, probably, in a second, everyone. So the round has impacted on his chest, it's now -- the gun is now pointing towards me, so again I'm thinking he's going to shoot me. So, again, because

52

I think Mr Duggan would have been falling backwards at that time.

THE ASSISTANT CORONER: You're focusing on him, you are looking at him all the time you are not looking away or blinking.

A. No.

THE ASSISTANT CORONER: Suddenly the gun disappears.

A. It did, sir, yes. Again, sir, it's happened so quick. If you imagine, this is happening in a split second, one second it was there and the next second when I looked thankfully he wasn't pointing at me.

THE ASSISTANT CORONER: What was he doing?

A. I think he was -- I can't remember exactly but he was falling backwards.

MR UNDERWOOD: Did he fall forwards first or did he fall backwards first?

A. Again, I cannot be precise because at that time I've given a big loud shout of "Shots fired, shots fired" because I wanted to let everyone know that I've actually engaged Mr Duggan and I just remember him falling backwards and officers converging on him.

Q. Is it your evidence, be clear about this, that he had the gun in his hand from the moment you saw him turn towards you?

A. Absolutely.

54

1  I've got an honest held belief he's going to shoot me or
2  one of my colleagues and I have reassessed the threat
3  and I've discharged a second round from my MP5, which
4  appeared to impact on his right arm -- or right bicep,
5  shall I say, sorry.
6  Q. Okay. Did you see how his jacket was being worn?
7  A. All I remember was his jacket was open.
8  Q. Would it be fair to say you were focused on the gun?
9  A. Again, the only way I can describe this is a freeze
10  frame moment, is where you are just focused on what's
11  going to cause you harm. Whereas initially I had lovely
12  vision, but once the gun is in Mark Duggan's hand, my
13  focus is just glued on the gun and what that gun is
14  going to do to me.
15  Q. How did it get over the railings?
16  A. I don't know, sir, I would love to be able to answer
17  that question.
18  Q. Help us as best you can.
19  THE ASSISTANT CORONER: Before that question -- I was hoping
20  the question might have been a bit more neutral: what
21  happened to the gun?
22  A. Sir, the next time I look to reassess, the gun wasn't
23  there. So in the course of like a split second, one
24  second the gun is there and the next second, when
25  I looked and reassessed the gun is not there because

53

1  Q. He had that gun in his hand while you fired both shots?
2  A. Absolutely.
3  Q. But it suddenly wasn't there?
4  A. Yes.
5  Q. Did you become aware that W42 had been shot?
6  A. Yes. After I said "Shots fired, shots fired", because
7  I'm a medic, my role then becomes to provide first aid,
8  because we've got a casualty now, the threat is
9  neutralised, in police terms but again -- in layman's
10  terms, there's no gun threat there at the minute. But
11  now we have a casualty, so my role as a medic is now to
12  provide first aid. However, at that time, W42 goes "I'm
13  hit, I'm hit".
14  Q. What did you do?
15  A. (Pause)
16  It's something that I'll never forget to be honest
17  because he's a mate of mine and I went over to him
18  and --
19  MR STERN: Sorry to interrupt but --
20  THE ASSISTANT CORONER: I think we might have a break now,
21  generally.
22  MR STERN: Whether we have a break or not, if people feel
23  they are not able to listen to this evidence -- this is
24  evidence that is anticipated in statements and indeed
25  heard before. If people feel they cannot listen to it,

55

## Contradictions

As we scoured the documents, we paid particular attention to points at which the available accounts, whether eyewitness testimony or expert evidence, diverged from one another. While small differences in a recollection of the same event, especially of intense situations, are a regular feature of testimony, some of the contradictions—especially between the accounts of the event given by V53 and those given by other officers—opened the possibility that V53's "honestly held belief" might not have been truthful.

For example, the officers' various accounts give two contradictory versions of what Duggan did as he exited the minicab. V53 claims that after stepping onto the pavement, Duggan initially turned and faced west along Ferry Lane toward W42 before turning 180 degrees to face him and W70, who stood beside him. And according to V53, it was only after Duggan had turned toward him that he saw the gun in Duggan's hand. But the testimonies of officers W42, W70, and R68—all of whom had a clear view of the moment of exit—all state that Duggan turned immediately toward V53 after

exiting. This apparently minor difference is important because it demonstrates that the scenario within which V53 claims he first saw the gun is itself disputed.

*Testimonies given by officers at the coroner's inquest.*
*Below: V53's account, given on 15 October 2013.*
*Opposite, clockwise from top: W42 (24 October 2013);*
*R68 (22 October 2013); and W70 (23 October 2013).*

```
 1   A.  Initially he was facing W42, so he was facing towards
 2       the general direction of where the Alpha car is.
 3   Q.  Just so we are all clear on this, this is looking
 4       towards the brow of the hill towards where the Tube
 5       station is?
 6   A.  Yes.
 7   Q.  So by the time you had got out of your vehicle, do you
 8       say Mark Duggan had gone in that general direction?
 9   A.  What I recall is he -- as I say he's jumped out, he's
10       facing W42, W42 shouts "Stand still" and he's facing him
11       but I don't think he moves from what I can recall, as in
12       any further steps, he sort of stood still, sees W42 and
13       stops.
14   Q.  So just pause there. So your evidence is he gets out --
15   A.  Yes.
16   Q.  -- but merely turns and is looking in the direction of
17       where W42 is?
18   A.  That's what I remember, sir, yes.
19   Q.  So your evidence isn't that he gets out and initially
20       goes towards W42?
21   A.  Again, sir, I can't say with 100 per cent certainty that
22       he took any steps but my recollection was that he faced
23       him and stopped. But, again, I cannot be 100 per cent
24       certain. He may have done a couple of steps, I don't
25       know, but my recollection, when I've seen him, when he
```

```
 1       jumped out, he stopped and he was facing W42.
 2   Q.  Yes. You see, on your version of events, when -- wha
 3       Mark Duggan has done is he's literally just -- howeve
 4       you want to put it -- jumped out of the vehicle and h
 5       on the pavement right by the taxi doors; is that righ
 6   A.  Yes. There or thereabouts, sir, yes.
 7   Q.  Just so we're clear, what you say is you say that you
 8       hear W42 say "Stand still"?
 9   A.  Yes. He initially shouted armed police when he was
10       within the cab --
11   Q.  Don't worry about the conversation for the moment. I
12       concentrating on the positioning. We'll come back to
13       the conversation in a moment.
14   A.  Okay.
15   Q.  He gets out, W42 says whatever W42 says?
16   A.  Yes.
17   Q.  Mark Duggan, on your version of events, doesn't appro
18       W42. All he does is he pivots round, correct?
19   A.  That's my recollection, sir, yes.
20   Q.  When he pivots round, it's not your evidence, is it,
21       that he makes any movement towards you, apart from
22       pivoting around?
23   A.  As I say, sir, at that time I don't remember because
24       obviously it happened so quickly but all I remember,
25       with certainty, is he's done a pivot, I don't know if
```

```
 1    you follow?  That's where I'm at.
 2  A.  Yes, no problem, sir.
 3  Q.  At any stage, when he steps out of the vehicle, does he
 4      turn and face you?
 5  A.  No, sir.
 6  Q.  Because you are in the direction of where the Alpha car
 7      is, aren't you?  The Alpha car is behind you -- you exit
 8      the Alpha car --
 9  A.  I do, yes.
10  Q.  -- so behind you is the Alpha car, correct?
11  A.  Correct, yes.
12  Q.  Do you follow what I'm saying?
13  A.  Yes, I follow, yes.
14  Q.  Just so we are absolutely crystal clear about your
15      account, you don't say at any stage Mark Duggan is
16      facing you or facing the direction of the Alpha vehicle?
17  A.  That's correct, yes.
18  Q.  Just so we are clear on this, you know behind your
19      vehicle is where the Tube station is, isn't it?
20  A.  Further up the road, yes.
21  Q.  Further up in that direction?
22  A.  Yes.
23  Q.  So, you see, again, can we just be clear on this: when
24      you say you see him from behind, the words you say you
25      use are "He's reaching".

                              73
```

```
 1      which direction was Mr Duggan?  Was he facing you or was
 2      he facing W42?
 3  A.  As I saw him emerge, he was facing -- it's quite hard to
 4      describe exactly how because he rolled out of the
 5      minicab so he was never looking in any particular
 6      direction for more than a split second but I did not see
 7      him look up towards W42.
 8  THE ASSISTANT CORONER:  Your evidence of pivoting, as
 9      I understand what you're saying, is virtually his left
10      shoulder really on the sliding door coming out and
11      coming straight in your direction; is that right?
12  A.  Exactly that, sir, yes.
13  THE ASSISTANT CORONER:  Thank you.
14  MR THOMAS:  So he pivots out of the vehicle immediately into
15      your direction, so he's then, as it were, face on with
16      you; would that be right?
17  A.  Yes, that's correct.
18  Q.  Can you just help us with this: just so I'm absolutely
19      clear as to what you are saying, as soon as he's out and
20      his feet are on the pavement and he's face on with you,
21      can you see the gun, at that point.  So he's literally
22      just stepped out of the vehicle, he's pivoted and he's
23      facing you; can you see the gun?
24  A.  My perception was, as he's turned -- as immediate -- as
25      I can tell, almost immediately he's just moved his lapel

                              80
```

```
 1      isn't that Mark gets out of the minicab, faces the
 2      direction towards the left and begins to make his way
 3      towards the left, is it?
 4  A.  No, sir.
 5  Q.  That would be quite wrong, would it, on your evidence,
 6      on your account?
 7  A.  I didn't see that, sir.
 8  Q.  Officer, I'm asking, you see him when he gets out of --
 9      you see when he puts his feet on the pavement and then
10      you have a clear and unobstructed view.  I'm just asking
11      you: on your account it would be quite wrong to suggest
12      Mark went in the direction of the left?
13  A.  I didn't see that, sir, no.
14  Q.  You didn't see that but you were in a position to see
15      that.  That's the point I'm making.
16  A.  Right, sir, I can only tell you what I saw, sir, I only
17      saw him move towards --
18  Q.  To the right?
19  A.  To the right, yes, sir.
20  Q.  On your version of events, Mark Duggan, when he gets out
21      of the cab, goes to the right --
22  A.  Yes, sir.
23  Q.  -- not to the left?
24  A.  No, sir.
25  Q.  Doesn't even face to the left?

                              81
```

## State-Sanctioned Coordination

Armed officers are required to follow certain procedures in the aftermath of a police shooting, including how to record their initial recollections of such an incident, and then how to do so again later in more detail. However, ambiguity in these guidelines leaves the opportunity for officers to intentionally coordinate details of their statements concerning the critical moments of the event.[4]

In this case, almost all of the available eyewitness evidence was given by individuals with a professional association with one another, and arguably with an interest in protecting one another. Truthful descriptions of an incident from multiple perspectives tend to converge and mutually support each other, but instances where multiple testimonies repeat a falsehood in a similar manner, as well as otherwise unusual synchronicity between testimonies, could point to coordination and raise questions about the integrity and honesty of the relevant accounts. For example, at least six officers described the minicab in which Duggan was traveling as "gold" in color, though it was silver. One of the officers admitted that when they gathered to write their detailed statements on 7 August, he wrote down key details on a flip chart for the benefit of the others, including, mistakenly, that the vehicle was "gold."[5]

In relation to the questions closer to the heart of the incident—such as how many shots were fired—at least five officers used precisely the same phrase in their EAB reports: "a number of shots." Notably, a sixth officer, Q63, began to write that he had perceived "two shots," getting as far as "two s-," before scribbling it out and also writing "a number of shots."[6] Socializing the process of recollecting the very moment of shooting contradicts the stated necessity that each officer should "individually record what their honestly held belief of the situation was at the time force was used."[7]

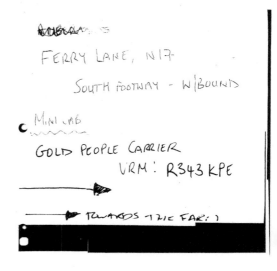

Top: Page from the flip chart on which officer V59 wrote down key details of the incident for the benefit of the officers who gathered to produce their detailed statements on 7 August 2011.
Bottom: The silver minicab.

The guidelines that allowed officers to confer, per protocol, on aspects of the case, were updated in 2019, after legal pressure from the family's lawyers led to a yearslong negotiation between the Independent Office of Police Complaints, the government, and the Metropolitan Police. Partially motivated by the Duggan case, these reforms nevertheless still failed to go as far as an outright ban on conferring.[8]

4. The guidelines in effect in 2011 for such incidents did state that, in general, officers "should not confer with others" in the process of writing up their accounts, but they permitted the practice in certain circumstances.
5. This detail emerged during V59's questioning at the inquest. See "Inquest into the Death of Mark Duggan: Transcript of the Hearing 9 October 2013," p. 78. Available at <bit.ly/3x1zXMP>.
6. While the benefit of making the number of shots ambiguous is not immediately apparent, it might have functioned at that stage as a way of leaving open the possibility that Duggan had also fired a shot, as the IPCC erroneously told the press shortly after the incident.

7. See "Manual of Guidance on the Management, Command and Deployment of Armed Officers," second edition, 2010, p. 118.
8. See Vikram Dodd, "Javid Accused of Giving Way to Police over No Conferring Rule," The Guardian, 17 January 2019. Available at <bit.ly/3prqyvz>. The IOPC's "Statutory Guidance to the Police Force on Achieving Best Evidence in Death and Serious Injury Matters," issued in January 2019, is available at <bit. ly/3fWxn4Y>. The College of Policing's guidance, issued in July 2020, is available at <bit.ly/3geQ8j3>.

Continued: was posted as the Back Seat operator (MARS). I was armed with a Glock 17 (34 rounds), a Taser with (2 rounds) and an MP5 which was slipped in the Boot of our car. We were engaged on a MAST operation. Whilst on route to the main briefing we received info to stop a Gold people carrier index R343KPE. An Armed Intervention was carried out in FERRY LA, near ——48 TOTTENHAM HALE N17 @ 1813hr. I deployed from my vehicle, was aware that shots had been fired. Rendered first aid to the subject who had been fatally wounded.

V48

Signature: V48

---

*...ers' accounts of the color of the vehicle, which they incorrectly ...ibe as gold. Clockwise from top: V48's EAB, written on ...ust 2011; V59's testimony at the coroner's inquest, 9 October ...V53's testimony at the inquest, 15 October 2013.*

distinctive due to its 'gold' like colour and mirror in its back window."

Officer, it was silver, wasn't it?

A. I don't know, sir. I would probably describe it as gold, to be honest with you, I recall.

Q. Let's take this in stages. First of all we know from ZZ37 that he described it as bronze; do you recall that?

A. No, sir, I don't.

Q. The commentary may well have had "bronze" in it; do you recall?

A. I don't recall, sir, no.

Q. "Gold" is used twice in the flip charts that V59 put together for the briefing on 7 August; do you recall that?

A. I do, sir, yes.

Q. Everybody seems to describe it either as bronze from that commentary or gold from the flip charts. I'll be corrected if I'm wrong by saying it's everybody but at least a large number of the officers making notes and making their statements on 7 August pick up that colour scheme.

A. Okay, sir.

Q. Now, you're saying, are you, that you remember it as being gold?

A. That's how I would describe it, sir, yes. It was

36

1  was posted to which vehicle, that sort of thing. There
2  was no opinion --
3  THE ASSISTANT CORONER: During these hours, you didn't say
4  "I saw this" and someone else said "No, I didn't see
5  that".
6  A. No, because we didn't discuss what someone saw or didn't
7  see. It was in relation to vehicle positioning,
8  sequence of events, the timings and those things are all
9  fairly -- they are factual, as opposed to opinions and
10  what an individual person has seen is individual to
11  them, it's their decision what they write in their
12  statement.
13  THE ASSISTANT CORONER: So, for example, a very small
14  example, is you just read out the fact you said it was
15  a bronze minicab.
16  A. Yes.
17  THE ASSISTANT CORONER: On your notes, you've written down
18  it's a gold minicab, and in your final statement
19  sometimes you call it gold sometimes you call it bronze.
20  A. Yes, I do.
21  THE ASSISTANT CORONER: Now, we are not Olympic athletes, it
22  does not matter whether it's bronze or gold to us. Was
23  there something like that going on and you were saying
24  "Perhaps I've got the colour wrong?"
25  A. No, I think that's my mistake really, I just decided to

142

Continued: Stop a gold people Carrier type Vehicle index R343 KPE. We made our way to the location and stopped the Vehicle in Ferry Lane N17. We stopped the Vehicle and deployed from our Vehicle. The Subject got out of the Vehicle. I ran towards the man as I did So I heard a number of Shots fired and Saw the man fall to the ground. A number of officers began to administer first aid. After a short period I began to search a small grassed area close to the incident. I found what appeared to be a Self loading pistol wrapped in a black Sock. I did not touch it. I arranged for a exhibit box to cover it and a plastic bag over that. After a short period of time I was relieved by a uniformed officer. After Short period of time we left the Scene

Signature: R31

The Evidence and Action Book reports of R31, Q63, and W39, all of whom describe hearing "a number of shots."

Continued: the Hutton Slot gin in conclusion two. At approximately 18·00 hours we were tasked to complete an armed Stop on a Vehicle index R343 KPE. At approximately 18·13 hours that Stop took place in Ferry Lane near to Tottenham Hale tube Station N17. R31 was operating, Q63 was driving. As our vehicle came to a Stop I deployed from Bravo. A number of Shots were fired, I Saw the Subject hit and W42 had been hit. First aid was given to both Parties. A short time later we left the Scene. W39

23:51 TH 4AUG'11 C013

W39

Signature: W39

Continued: 11·00hrs. At about 18:00hrs we were asked to carry out a stop on a people carrier, index R343KPE as it was believed that the occupant of the vehicle was in possession of a firearm. We located the vehicle in Ferry Lane and at about 18:13hrs a non-compliant stop was implemented. As I ran towards the rear of the vehicle I heard a number of Shots being fired and saw a black male fall to the floor. A police officer had also been shot. I co-ordinated other resources whilst first aid was given. I then videoed 1st Aid of the Black male until life was pronounced extinct. I then left the scene. Q63

23:36 TH 4AUG'11 C013

Q63

Signature: Q63

Q. What is important when the witness gives their evidence
1
2    is their perception; do you agree?
3  A. What I've heard is two bangs which is potentially
4    a number of shots.
5  Q. Officer, what you need to recall in your evidence is
6    what you witness, what you perceived. Why didn't you
7    write this: I heard two bangs, which could have been
8    a number of shots? Help us.
9  A. Because I just put "a number of shots".
10 Q. You see, there's a curious thing here. You then
11   subsequently change the two bangs, when you come to make
12   your later statement from "a number of shots" to "two
13   shots"?
14 A. That's probably right because later on I actually know
15   that to be definitely the case.
16 Q. How do you know it to be definitely the case? Who told
17   you that was definitely the case? There had been no
18   investigation, the investigation hadn't been completed
19   then?
20 A. I don't know who told me.
21 Q. No, but you have just said that by the time you came to
22   make your statement three days later on 7 August, you
23   knew that to be definitely the case. The IPCC hadn't
24   conducted their investigation, it had not been concluded
25   so; how did you know?

141

Excerpts from the same three officers' testimonies at the coroner's inquest concerning the number of shots they heard at the time. Clockwise from top: The testimony of R31, 10 October 2013; Q63, 10 October 2013, and W39, 22 October 2013.

1    training, and that a number of shots didn't quantify
2    what had happened, to give myself the correct amount of
3    time to see the full recollection of the whole event not
4    just that one individually that was sufficient to
5    explain what I had seen.
6  Q. Did you actually need time to recall that it was two
7    shots? If somebody had said to you, "Look, how many
8    shots were there?", would you have said two?
9  A. I would have said I thought it was two, yes --
10   I thought. That's what we worked (?) right on
11   an initial account.
12 MR UNDERWOOD: Thank you very much. Wait there, please.
13 THE ASSISTANT CORONER: Yes, Mr Thomas?
14          Questions by MR THOMAS
15 MR THOMAS: W39, I represent the loved ones of Mark Duggan.
16 A. Sir.
17 Q. Why not just simply say in your initial account
18   "I thought it was two shots"; you could have done that?
19 A. I could have done that, sir.
20 Q. Why not do that?
21 A. I had not been involved in one of these situations
     before, a shooting before. I was 99 per cent sure it
     was two shots. I don't know how I react after the
     48 hours rest period before making my recollection.
     I believe the number of shots covered that and that's

128

1    was in, if you could.
2  A. He was standing for sure. He was bent slightly forward,
3    I suggest, as though he was -- had been or was running.
4    It was a snapshot I saw but he was lent slightly forward
5    and was moving towards the officers which were deploying
6    from our Charlie vehicle.
7  Q. Could you see his arms?
8  A. I couldn't, no.
9  Q. You say it's a snapshot; was it just a glimpse?
10 A. Absolutely, yes.
11 Q. Did you hear shots?
12 A. I did, yes.
13 Q. What happened then?
14 A. As I got really -- between really our Bravo vehicle and
15   the Charlie vehicle, the front of that, I hadn't quite
16   reached the pavement. I know that for a fact, and
17   I heard two shots and I saw Mr Duggan, I would describe
18   it as buckle slightly at the waist, as though he had
19   been wounded -- sorry, winded not "wounded", as if
20   somebody had perhaps -- you know, he had been punched in
21   the stomach. It had that kind of effect where he bent
22   forward.
23 Q. Did he come back up?
24 A. I do not believe he did, no.
25 Q. Let's get this clear: he slightly stooped forward as if

158

59

1 to give yourself that little bit of time overnight or

2 48 hours before you confirmed it; that's what you just

3 told us, correct?

4 A. That's true, sir, yes.

5 Q. May I suggest the real reason for not putting the numb

6 of shots is you knew, because you were at the scene an

7 you knew that Mark Duggan had been shot, you were full

8 aware that there were two injuries to Mark Duggan, his

9 arm and the injury to his chest. But you also knew th

10 a colleague had been shot. So there was the possibil

11 that three shots may have been discharged; is that the

12 real reason why you and your colleagues were reluctant

13 to put down the number of shots on the night?

14 A. I wasn't aware how many times Mr Duggan had been hit a

15 that stage. I was aware W42 had been hit because of

16 what he said to me and -- sorry, I cannot recall the

17 second part of your question.

18 Q. My suggestion to you is: the real reason why you and

19 your colleagues -- let's just focus on you. You were

20 reluctant to put the true number of shots down because

21 you didn't know what V53 was going to say.

22 A. Sir, that is ridiculous.

23 Q. All right. Let me move on.

24 Can we call up, please, your witness statement of

25 7 August. It's at page 158, please, in the witness

135

The inquest referred to two documents—the Evidence and Action Books and the "Manual of Guidance on the Management, Command and Deployment of Armed Officers"—that outlined the protocols that the CO19 team should have followed when writing their reports of the shooting. Both use ambiguous language that gives officers latitude to confer on certain aspects of the incident.

This page: W39 questioned during his testimony on 22 October 2013 about what subjects the officers had conferred on while writing their reports.

1 statement bundle. Can we just go to the last page,

2 which is 162. Can we just expand that, please?

3 This is what you say. By the time you write this

4 full statement -- do you see that?

5 A. Sorry, sir, this is the typed version, I've seen that.

6 I am just checking to make sure it's --

7 THE ASSISTANT CORONER: Please check it, yes.

8 A. (Pause)

9 Yes, sir.

10 MR THOMAS: By the time you write the detailed account on

11 7 August, the one officer who is now present with you is

12 V53.

13 A. He was there, sir, yes.

14 Q. Yes. So that's the difference between the 4th and the

15 7th you have now got V53 sitting in with you?

16 A. That's the difference with who was there, yes.

17 Q. Secondly, you say this. Again, if you just follow:

18 "I conferred with these officers on [the following

19 matters]: road names, routes, times and chronology."

20 A. Yes, sir.

21 Q. Did you confer on anything else?

22 A. No, sir?

23 Q. Can you help me with this: your pocket book, what we

24 have just been looking at, there is no mention, is there

25 of the colour of the minicab, is there?

136

1 A. There isn't, sir, no.

2 Q. By the time you make your witness statement, you would

3 agree with this: there's no doubt about it the minicab

4 is silver.

5 A. I haven't seen it since, sir, no.

6 Q. Can we just call up a photo of the minicab, any one wi

7 do.

8 A. It looks silver, sir, yes.

9 Q. It looks silver, doesn't it, and it is silver?

10 A. It is, yes.

11 Q. Just help me with this. There's no mention of the

12 colour of the minicab in your initial account. We the

13 get to the 4th, your detailed account, and if we turn

14 page 159, at the bottom, last paragraph, five lines f

15 the bottom, you describe the minicab as a "gold-colou

16 people vehicle"; do you see that?

17 A. I do, sir, yes.

18 Q. Where do you get the colour gold from? Because

19 according to your statement this isn't one of the thi

20 you confer on?

21 A. Sir, first of all the things we conferred on was writ

22 on a flip chart, which I believe has been exhibited,

23 I am not sure who by but I believe -- V59, was it? Y

24 The colour of the minicab and the index was on that.

25 did confer on that. It's correct, my statement does

137

NOT PROTECTIVELY MARKED | Manual of Guidance on the Management, Command and
Deployment of Armed Officers, Second Edition
7: Post Deployments

7: Post Deployments

these services, investigating officers, Post Incident Managers and staff association representatives have distinct roles. It is, however, essential that all officers, Post Incident Managers and those involved in any debriefing process are able to demonstrate integrity of purpose in all communications between each other and in record making and debrief procedures.

7.86 All appropriate steps should be taken by the Police Service in the initial stages following the discharge of firearms to reduce any possible risks of the investigation, required under Article 2 ECHR, being undermined by any deficiencies, such as failing to secure the evidence, including witness testimony and forensic evidence. The procedures adopted should be designed so as to demonstrate integrity of purpose in all actions and discussions between the officers involved.

7.87 Nothing in this section should be interpreted as constraining effective action by the Police Service or the officers involved in adopting an operationally necessary procedure to secure best evidence, arrest or bring to justice those who may be involved in ongoing criminal activity, or a follow-up investigative process.

7.88 The responsibility for securing evidence and taking appropriate action in an Article 2 investigation remains with the Police Service until such time as the independent investigative authority has taken over the investigation.

7.89 The responsibility of the police force being investigated is to facilitate that investigation through, for example:

- Identification and preservation of scenes and exhibits;
- Identification of immediately available witnesses;
- Securing of physical evidence;
- The availability of experienced family or witness liaison officers.

7.90 Early notification to the independent investigative authority will enable these procedures to be adopted, and initial actions being taken by the police to be agreed at an early stage.

**Providing Accounts**

7.91 Where an initial account is made by officers, it should, subject to any legal advice that they are given, be made as soon as practicable. These accounts should be recorded in writing, timed, dated and signed.

7.92 Each officer's initial account should only consist of their individual recollection of events and should, among other things, address the question of what they believed to be the facts and why, if relevant, they considered that the use of force and discharge of firearms was absolutely necessary.

7.93 Detailed accounts should not normally be made immediately, but can be left until the officers involved in the shooting are better able to articulate their experience in a coherent format, normally after at least forty-eight hours.

7.94 As a matter of general practice, officers should not confer with others before making their accounts (whether initial or subsequent accounts). The important issue is to individually record what their honestly held belief of the situation was at the time force was used. There should, therefore, be no need for an officer to confer with others about what was in their mind at the time force was used. If, however, in a particular case a need to confer on other issues does arise, then, in order to ensure transparency and maintain public confidence, where some discussion has taken place, officers must document the fact that this has taken place, highlighting:

- Time, date and place where conferring took place;
- The issues discussed;
- With whom;
- The reasons for such discussion.

7.95 There is a positive obligation on officers involved to ensure that all activity relating to the recording of accounts is transparent and capable of withstanding scrutiny.

7.96 Where an officer has any concerns that the integrity of the process is not being maintained, they must immediately draw this to the attention of the person in charge of the post incident process and ensure that this is documented.

7.97 A person involved in a traumatic or life-threatening encounter will often experience a range of physiological and psychological responses which may determine their perception of time, distance, auditory and visual stimuli and the chronology of key events. This may affect their ability immediately after the incident to recall what may be important detail. Where, over time, officers recall further information, this should be recorded in a further account.

7.98 There may be circumstances where it is necessary for officers to provide more detailed information at an earlier stage. This could be to address issues associated with a person who is now in custody, or in relation to an ongoing criminal investigation, for example, where a person was not arrested at the scene.

7.99 It is the responsibility of each individual police officer involved in the incident to ensure that any information that may be relevant to the investigation is revealed, recorded and retained. This information should include an officer's own observations relating to the incident and any accounts received from witnesses.

CD010958

CD010959

---

31

## NOTES OF ARREST/REPORT OF INCIDENT

TIME NOTES STARTED: **2322**

TIME NOTES COMPLETED: **0010**

LOCATION NOTES MADE: **HO**

PERSONS PRESENT............

It is essential that you record a complete account of events. It is intended to protect you from needless civil action or complaint investigation. You MUST follow the following guidance. Your notes will be subject to close scrutiny. You may confer with other officers who were present for an overview, but these notes are to assist YOUR recollection.

**Background**

- Set the scene:  As fully as possible "on day, date, time, place, etc."
- State the information you had before attending the scene, this will help explain your actions.
- If notes were not made at scene, explain fully.
- Do not mention sensitive sources/techniques.

**Action**

- State what happened when you arrived.
- Record all questions asked/answers given both before and after caution. **Keep an open mind.** You are duty bound to gather all evidence and entitled to question any person from whom useful information can be obtained. **You should include hearsay.**
- Fully record your actions and the options considered up to the point of arrest.
- Show what factors influenced your decision, include reasons for *not* taking action.

continued on next page

*Top: Pages from the 2010 edition of the "Manual of Guidance on the Management, Command and Deployment of Armed Officers" outlining the official policy for how officers should provide accounts after an incident involving the use of firearms.*
*Bottom: Front cover of an Evidence and Action Book with guidance on conferring.*

## Spatialization: Part 1

In order to evaluate the officers' testimonies, we used a spreadsheet to divide the incident into nine distinct stages—such as "minicab stops," "Mark Duggan begins to exit," "first shot," "between shots," "second shot," and "after the shots"—that closely track the freeze-frame moments in their accounts. We repeated this process for each officer, as well as for the expert reports and the testimony of the minicab driver.[9] The result was a textual matrix of more than a hundred cells, each with a short narrative description of a particular moment in the incident seen through the eyes of one individual.

We then modeled the cells that contained spatial information, allowing us to examine them against other evidence. Superimposing the different models began to reveal information regarding the probable relative location of the people and objects involved in the incident, as well as critical differences between accounts. Analyses of spatial and material evidence provided objective facts against which we could determine the accuracy of the officers' descriptions.

|  | 1<br>Minicab stops | 2<br>M.D. begins to exit | 3<br>M.D. turns | 4<br>M.D. faces V53 | 5<br>Before first shot | 6<br>First shot | 7<br>Between shots | 8<br>Second shot | 9<br>After the shots |
|---|---|---|---|---|---|---|---|---|---|
| **W70** | | | | | | | | | |
| **V53** | | | | | | | | | |
| **W42** | | | | | | | | | |
| **Q63** | | | | | | | | | |
| **R31** | | | | | | | | | |
| **W39** | | | | | | | | | |
| **R68** | | | | | | | | | |
| **V59** | | | | | | | | | |
| **W56** | | | | | | | | | |

*Detail from spreadsheet used to spatialize the various textual descriptions of the incident.*

9. We also studied the testimony of a member of the public known as Witness B, whose importance to the case will be discussed in more detail later.

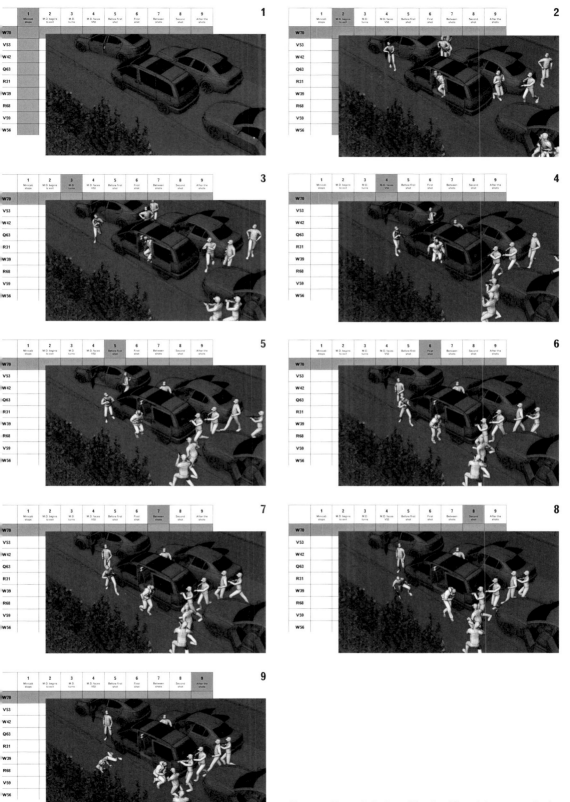

*This page: The spatialization of the nine different stages according to W70's description of the incident.*

63

## Spatialization: Part 2

Spatial reconstructions of cases extend across three layers: "site," "scene," and "incident." The site layer includes the static environment or urban fabric — buildings, roads, vegetation — in and around which the event unfolded. The scene layer includes the organization of the larger nonhuman elements, which in the Duggan case consisted of the location of the five vehicles. Finally, the incident layer includes the dynamic elements of an event — people's positions, perspectives, movements, and actions, as well as moving objects such as bullets or a gun being thrown.

The site layer remained largely unchanged between 2011 and 2018, when we began our work on the case. To reconstruct this layer in digital space, we used photogrammetry, a computational process that translates a large multiplicity of photographs of the same space from different directions into an accurately measurable and geo-referenced 3D model. Small variations in perspective between sequences of images allow the relative dimensions of objects and environments to be determined with precision: we therefore moved incrementally across the site, taking photographs every half-meter from a high, medium, and low viewpoint, in such a way that the field of view of each photograph overlapped with that of others in the series. Since photogrammetry cannot give absolute measurements, we needed to calibrate, or "ground truth," the model by measuring the width of a paving slab and the height of a fence, and we then scaled the model accordingly.

The only difference between 2011 and the present was the state of the vegetation, which was important in that it could have affected differently what was and was not visible in the grassy area where the officers said they found the gun. We removed the present scan of vegetation from our photogrammetry model and reconstructed it using photographs from the day. We then reconstructed the scene layer — the positions of the four police vehicles and the minicab — based on aerial photographs taken from a police helicopter, which are in the public domain.

More precise information on the locations of the vehicles was available through a LIDAR scan carried out by the Metropolitan Police.[10] However, while we had access to these files during the investigation, the police denied us permission to use this data in any public presentation of this work, such as in the video investigation we have online, or in this book. Once the civil case for which we were originally commissioned was settled out of court, the Metropolitan Police's lawyers sent us a letter threatening legal action if we did not delete the file from our server. We did so in the presence of our lawyer, David Kuper.

10. LIDAR, which stands for Light Detection and Ranging, a remote-sensing method that uses light in the form of a pulsed laser to measure distances.

## Situation Plans

As part of the IPCC's investigation, the officers were asked to annotate plan views of the scene, indicating the various areas within which they believed V53, Duggan, W42, and others, including themselves, had been positioned in the moments before, during, and after the shooting.

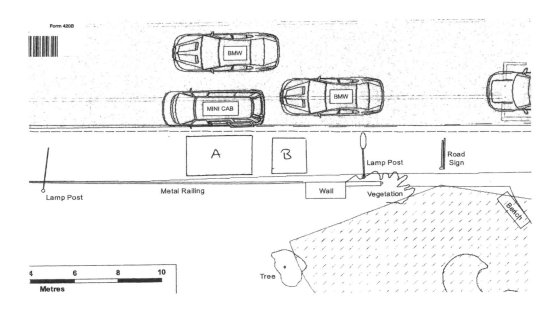

*Above and opposite: Images National Archives.*

By overlaying and cross-referencing these plans, we arrived at zones of higher probability for the locations of V53 and W42, at the time of the first and second shots. We then cross-referenced these diagrams with the written descriptions given by the officers, tentatively excluding areas of the plans that did not accord with multiple officers' spatial descriptions and with material evidence recorded on-site. We also excluded parts of the areas drawn by the officers that we determined were functionally impossible given the various actors' necessary lines of sight relative to the incident's position within the site and the scene.

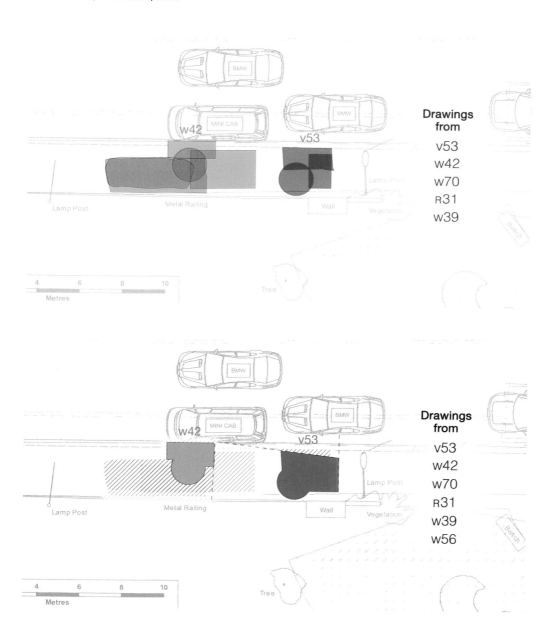

Drawings
from

v53
w42
w70
R31
w39

Drawings
from

v53
w42
w70
R31
w39
w56

## Shot Lines

Pathology reports commissioned as part of the civil case helped us to determine more precisely the relative locations of Duggan, W42, and V53 at the time of the first shot, and the positions of Duggan and V53 relative to the minicab door at the time of the second shot.

In consultation with Professor Derrick Pounder—the forensic pathologist for the IPCC investigation who had since been commissioned by the Duggan family's legal team in the context of the civil suit—we created a precise 3D model of Duggan's body, including the location of the gunshot wounds.

The first shot, according to Pounder, went through Duggan's right bicep, grazing the right-hand side of his chest; the second shot passed through his chest, exiting through the lower left-hand side of his back.

The locations of these wounds allowed us to draw "shot lines," which gave us highly accurate information about Duggan's body position during those moments. After passing through Duggan's right arm, the first shot hit W42's concealed underarm radio. (This shot may have led the IPCC to erroneously report that Duggan had shot at the police.) This information allowed us to extend the first shot line from the barrel of V53's weapon to W42's armpit.[11] Somewhere along that line was Duggan.

The second bullet—the lethal shot, which passed through Duggan's chest—was ultimately found on the floor of the minicab, allowing us to extend the second shot line from V53's weapon to Duggan's body. From the exit wound, we then extended a cone toward the open door of the minicab, the cone accounting for the possibility that the trajectory of a bullet might be altered by traversing a body.

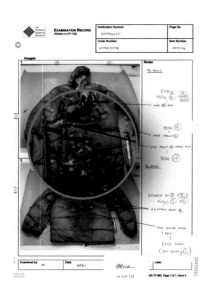

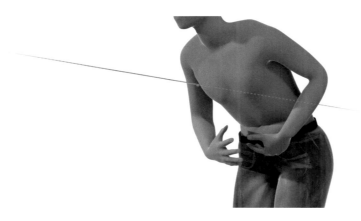

Modeling Duggan's jacket as a dynamic surface, which moved and flexed in relation to his body movements, gave us more details about his position. Two holes near the left-hand pocket might otherwise have appeared strange given that they were made by one shot, but they suggested that the jacket was folded back on itself at the time of the second shot—crucially, with his left hand across his chest. This observation implies that Duggan, having been hit in the right arm by the first shot, brought his left hand, which was in his jacket's left pocket, up toward the injury before the second shot passed through his jacket and impacted his chest.

The reconstruction—constituted by the shot lines and the damage to Duggan's jacket—runs counter to V53's recollection during the inquest of the sequence of the shots, in which he claimed that it was his first shot that had hit Duggan in the chest. In support of their self-defense claims, UK police officers have to account for every shot they fire in a given incident. When two shots have been fired, the second may be harder to defend in court, as the officer would need to convince the jury that he had an honest belief that the person still posed a danger even after the first shot. If the first shot had been the lethal one, then the second shot would have made little difference—you can't kill a dead man—and so there would have been no need to defend it.

V53's testimony contradicts Pounder's assessment with regard to the order of the shots. If V53's perception, recollection, or description of the event is demonstrably wrong in this regard, the IPCC had a basis for questioning the rest of his testimony, including his claim that he had seen the gun in the first place.

11. At the inquest, V53 described himself as being six feet, two inches tall, and W42 as approximately "five or six inches" shorter. See "Inquest into the Death of Mark Duggan: Transcript of the Hearing 15 October 2013," p. 58. Available at <bit.ly/3g9vNvy>.

## Motion

With the help of Pounder, we produced an animation of Duggan's movements in the moments before the shots. Pounder described how he could reconstruct something of Duggan's movements by reading the wounds. After exiting the minicab, Duggan turned immediately toward V53, an assessment that is at odds with the officer's account.[12] His left hand was in his left pocket, with his right hand across his waist. Duggan began to move with his right foot, traveling away from the minicab, according to Pounder's estimation, at an angle of approximately 22 degrees. He was struck by the first bullet as his left foot followed his right. His right foot then came across his left as he stumbled, his left arm moving up across his chest. This pulled his jacket upward and doubled it over in front of his torso, which was bent substantially forward as he was hit by the second bullet. This too does not agree with V53's description of Duggan pointing the gun toward him as he shot a second time.

One of our researchers recreated the first part of this sequence while wearing a motion capture suit, disembarking from an approximated "minicab door" and moving according to the sequence of actions stipulated by Pounder.[13] These movements, which the motion tracking software would translate into digital motion, tested in real space Pounder's report and brought a degree of natural human movement to our animation of Duggan's steps in the moments before the first shot.

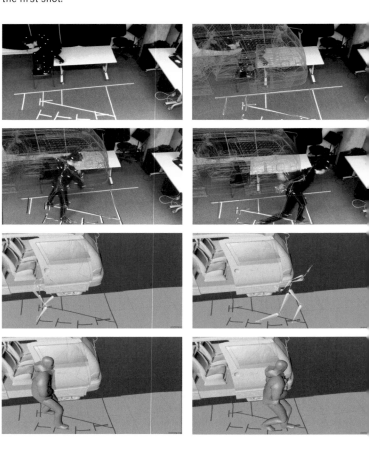

12. V53 is the only witness to describe Duggan as turning fully toward W42 and standing face-to-face with him before turning and moving toward him and W70.

13. "Motion capture" is a method for capturing all or part of an individual's physical movements in such a way that they can be translated into the action of a computer-generated 3D "character."

00:74 seconds

01:50 seconds

There will always be a margin of error involved in the process of estimating locations of individuals through such an interconnected network of evidentiary approaches. But the process of careful cross-referencing of testimonial, pathological, spatial, and physical evidence such as the location of blood splatter produces an evidentiary fabric, one in which all the pieces of evidence are tightly interwoven. In this way, the individual pieces adjust to one another until this evidentiary fabric, which began as an elastic entity, gradually coheres, increasing the probability that a given account is correct and reducing the margin of error. Our analysis also estimated the likely duration of the incident: from Duggan exiting the minicab to his receiving the second, fatal shot, no more than one and a half seconds had elapsed.

## A Thrown Gun?

Using this information, we were able to interrogate the possible routes by which the gun got to the grass. The first route, favored by the IPCC, is that Duggan threw the gun as he was struck by the second shot: "The most plausible explanation for the location of the firearm, JMA/1, is that Mr Duggan was in the process of throwing the firearm, JMA/1, to his right as he was shot."[14]

The IPCC's explanation for the reported location of the gun requires both Duggan to have been physically capable of throwing it during the period of the shots and V53 to have failed to see the movement. In order to test this assumption within our model, we added into our animated sequence a reconstruction of the physical movement that would have been required for Duggan to throw the gun to where it was found. The gun weighed just over one kilogram, and was found seven meters from where Duggan would have been standing at the time of the first shot.[15] A new biomechanical study by Dr. Jeremy J. Bauer, commissioned by the Duggan family's lawyers for the civil suit, showed that to travel that far, the gun would have had to leave Duggan's hand at about 6.7 meters per second at an angle of between 31 and 40 degrees.[16] The study concluded that "had Mr. Duggan tossed a gun over the fence, he would have had to toss the gun directly to his right side [...], with a large sweeping motion of his arm, or with a motion consistent with throwing a flying disc, or 'Frisbee.'"[17]

When on location with the lawyers representing the family, we sought to experience for ourselves the strength and movement necessary for such a throw, with a one-kilogram bag of sugar standing in for the gun. While this was not an exercise designed to develop formal evidence, it was important for us and for the lawyers who would be arguing the case to experience the relevant action with our own bodies.[18]

14. IPCC, "The Fatal Police Shooting of Mr Mark Duggan on 4 August 2011," p. 485. Available at <bit.ly/3geSZsm>.

15. The IPCC report on the killing describes the gun as being found only 4.35 meters away from Duggan's body, which is somewhat misleading. After he was shot, Duggan fell forward onto the ground and was subsequently rolled over onto his back to receive medical attention, both actions reducing the distance between him and the location at which the gun was found.

16. Jeremy J. Bauer, "Report on the Death of Mark Duggan" (2019), p. 14. Available at <bit.ly/3xYVbeQ>.

17. Ibid., p. 13.

18. In this way, the case echoed our 2016 investigation of the connections between a German secret service agent and the killing of a Turkish-German man, Halit Yozgat, by neo-Nazis. The agent denied that he had witnessed the killing, despite being seated only meters away. Halit's father, Ismail, asked the judges presiding over the murder trial to visit the scene of the killing in person: if they did so, he said, they would see immediately that the agent's testimony was false.

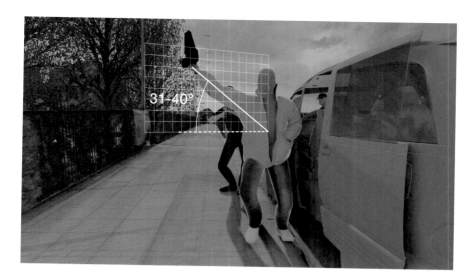

31-40°

6.7 m/s

At the inquest, V53 described Duggan's gun in detail: "I can make out the trigger guard, I can make out the barrel, and it's side-on to his body and there's a black sock covering that weapon."[19] Later, V53 told the inquest that his "focus [was] just glued on the gun." But he also said that he didn't see Duggan throwing the gun: "It would clear up a hell of a lot of stuff if I was able to say 'Yes, I saw the gun fly through the air and it landed wherever,' but I didn't see it."

Our analysis determined that V53 was likely standing just over three meters away from Duggan, looking directly at him. If he could describe the gun in such detail, is it possible that he missed it being thrown? What would the scene look like from V53's perspective?

By locating a "camera" at the position of V53's eyes, we could recreate an approximation of the view that he would have had at the moment of the shooting—the moment, or freeze-frame, on which the case hung.

19. "Inquest into the Death of Mark Duggan: Transcript of the Hearing 15 October 2013," p. 46. The following two quotes in this paragraph are from the same document, pp. 53 and 168, respectively.

## Cone of Vision

V53's defense of his actions is rooted in his privileged access to his own perceptions: according to the rules of the coroner's inquest, and in the eyes of the IPCC, *what he said he saw* is indisputable, an indivisible piece of evidence. While for the purposes of the inquest the jury needed only to be convinced that V53 held an "honest belief" that there was a gun in Duggan's hand at the time of the shots, the civil lawsuit demanded a higher standard of proof: that V53 had reasonable grounds to believe what he did. Given the significance of his visual field for the case, we needed to get as close to his experience as technology would allow.

The human field of vision is not like what we see on a two-dimensional screen. Human binocular vision has a wide field, which spans about 150 degrees horizontally and 130 degrees vertically.[20] We also need to consider the fact that our sensitivity to changes within that field of vision is not uniform: only in about 5 degrees of the field—the central area, that which we are looking directly toward —is the eye sufficiently sensitive for demanding visual-perceptual tasks, whereas marginal areas of the visual field are particularly sensitive to movement.[21] In order to further explore and evaluate V53's claims in regard to his perception of the gun, and the required throw, we recreated our animated sequence within an immersive virtual reality environment that simulates such aspects of human vision in a more natural way.

Peripheral vision

Central vision

Peripheral vision

20. Harry Moss Traquair, *An Introduction to Clinical Perimetry* (London: Henry Kimpton, 1938), pp. 4–5.

21. Stephen Pheasant and Christine M. Haslegrave, *Bodyspace: Anthropometry, Ergonomics and the Design of Work*, (Boca Raton: CRC Press, 1996), p. 63.

At the request of the family's legal team, we prepared a letter to the court explaining why VR provided the best means available to experience the scene and to evaluate the reasonability of V53's testimony. Virtual reality environments offer the opportunity for investigators, prosecutors, judges, and juries to cautiously step into the closest estimation possible of the private realm of an officer's perceptions. At the time the case was settled, Forensic Architecture was preparing its VR environment for the courtroom, in what would have been the first instance of this technology being used in the UK legal system.

### Biomechanics

According to both Pounder and Bauer, it is unlikely that after the first shot Duggan could have physically performed the motion required to throw the gun to where it was found.

Pounder wrote: "I cannot conceive of how MD could have thrown the Bruni gun forwards and to his right in an arc over fencing to where it is said to have been found."[22] And Bauer similarly concluded that "it was unlikely Mr. Duggan could have thrown the gun after he was shot in the arm. Instead, had he been holding a gun when he was shot, he likely would have dropped the gun where he was shot."[23]

22. Derrick Pounder, "Report on the Death of Mark Duggan" (2019), p. 19. Available at <bit.ly/3gWHCXp>.
23. Jeremy J. Bauer, "Report on the Death of Mark Duggan, p. 14.

## Reconstructing the Hard Stop

If Duggan didn't throw the gun at that time, there are only two remaining alternatives: either he threw it as he exited the minicab, or it was moved by police officers after the shooting and planted in the grass. Crucially, in both of these other scenarios, Duggan was not holding a gun when he was shot, and therefore posed no threat to the police.

In 2014, the jury in the coroner's inquest concluded that it was "more likely than not that Mark Duggan threw the firearm as soon as the minicab came to a stop."[24] This conclusion is not only a claim about Duggan's actions, but also about the perception of several officers: If Duggan had thrown the gun at this point, would it have passed through the field of vision of any of the officers?

24. See "Inquest Touching upon the Death of Mark Duggan," p. 3. Available at <bit.ly/3v0Ouqu>.

In order to explore this question, we needed to evaluate where the officers were positioned, and their fields of vision, at the time the jury suggested Duggan threw the gun. But we first had to understand how the "hard stop"—the maneuver by which the three undercover police cars surrounded the minicab —could have played out. At the coroner's inquest, a video was shown of the CO19 officers practicing just such a maneuver. Multiple officers from the unit described the hard stop on Ferry Lane as a "textbook"

procedure, and so we took the vehicle movements and timings from the training video and applied them to our animated model. (The rear windows of the minicab, a Toyota Previa, do not open, so Duggan could not have thrown the gun until the car had come to a stop and he had opened the door.)

## Officers' Perspectives

While all nine officers who exited their cars could have potentially noticed this throw, we identified four who would have been best positioned to notice the gun if it had been thrown at the moment that Duggan exited the vehicle: V53, W42, W70, and W56. None of these officers said they saw the gun being thrown in their written statements or their inquest testimonies. Indeed, W42 told the inquest: "There is no way Mark Duggan could have thrown the gun from the minicab and me not see it."[25]

V53 said that he watched the door of the minicab slide open and kept his eyes on the open door, which meant that the gun would have had to pass directly across the center of his field of vision. W70 exited from the same vehicle as V53, and would have had a similar view of the minicab. W56 told the inquest that as he moved around his car toward the minicab, he could see its driver looking over his left shoulder in the direction of Duggan. He also told the inquest that he could not see Duggan, but that he was looking in the direction of the left rear door, located on the opposite side of the minicab from where he stood. Despite not being able to see Duggan, his gaze was reportedly directed at the area that the gun would have needed to pass through, and he is therefore one of the best candidates to have seen it thrown.

25. See "Inquest into the Death of Mark Duggan: Transcript of the Hearing 24 October 2013," p. 66. Available at <bit.ly/3imEZiQ>.

*Clockwise from top left: The perspectives of officers W56, V53, W42, and W70, respectively, if Duggan had thrown the gun from the threshold of the minicab.*

The verdict of the inquest jury—a conclusion rejected by the IPCC—requires not just one but at least four officers to have failed to notice the gun being thrown.

The reconstruction of what these officers could have seen is best experienced in the online video of our investigation, where we show that the gun could potentially have crossed each of their fields of vision. As we are all anecdotally aware, that an object passes through one's field of vision does not guarantee that one notices it. But, in this instance, it does suggest that the officers could have noticed it. That being the case, with every additional officer who failed to notice it, the probability of this scenario is significantly reduced.

## Witness B

Finally, we considered the third option: that the gun was moved by police officers to the location at which they claimed to have found it.

The aftermath of the shooting was filmed from the ninth floor of a nearby residential building by a member of the public known as Witness B, who recorded seven videos on his Blackberry phone, totaling around fifteen minutes. The first of these clips begins approximately forty seconds after Duggan was shot, and it continues until after the police retrieve the gun from the grass. (It was first provided to a reporter at the BBC, and was thus subsequently referred to in some places as the "BBC footage.") Like the other six videos, this footage is grainy and low resolution. It captures almost the entirety of the scene, but indistinctly; individual officers are almost impossible to tell apart, and routinely fall out of sight behind the vehicles.

Witness B

It was on the basis of this footage that the IPCC rejected the possibility that the gun had been planted, saying that "there is also no sign of any officer planting a firearm on the grass during the 'BBC Footage'" and that there is no evidence any person entered the rear of the minicab."[26] We examined each of these claims in detail. The IPCC's first claim—that there is "no sign of any officer planting a firearm"—contains the implicit assumption that such an action, had it taken place, could be seen in the footage. But if such an action could not in any case be seen in such low-resolution footage, then the claim is meaningless. Would it ever be possible to see a handgun in such footage at so great a distance from the camera? To test this, we introduced a 1:1 model of the firearm into Witness B's footage at a point between the minicab and the location at which it was later found. Then we applied filters to it so that the gun's resolution matched the native resolution of the footage. The results demonstrated that the gun, or indeed any object the size of the gun, would not be clearly visible in the video at that distance.

26. IPCC, "The Fatal Police Shooting of Mr Mark Duggan n 4 August 2011," pp. 482 and 490, respectively.

*Above: Tracking the movement of officers frame-by-frame through the "BBC footage."*

## White Shadows

The IPCC's second claim about the footage—that there is "no evidence any person entered the rear of the minicab"—required more work to unpack. The open door of the minicab faced onto the pavement, hidden from Witness B's camera position, meaning that anybody who did access its rear seat—where Duggan had the gun as he was traveling toward Tottenham—would have disappeared from Witness B's footage before they did so.

To interrogate the IPCC's claim, then, we needed to track the officers as they moved around the scene in order to identify when any officer moved into the areas that would have been hidden from Witness B's camera: the "blind zones." We assigned a code name to each visible officer until we could work out who they were, if indeed we could. Some officers were more easily identifiable than others; for example, the officer known as Q63 stands out because of his white T-shirt.

The results of this tracking process were collated in a complex tracking chart (overleaf). Each row in the chart corresponds to an individual visible in the scene, but there are many more rows than there were individuals present. This is because we could often only track an individual for a short period, until they disappeared into one of the blind zones. Because of the number of people moving around the scene, and the concentration of activity around the minicab and police cars, it was often not possible to be sure that an individual who entered a blind zone was the same as the next officer observed leaving that same blind zone.

In some cases, it was also possible to cross-reference information from officers' testimonies with movements observed in the footage and identify one or more officers. As such, the lower bars of the tracking chart are given over to individuals whose identities were (sometimes briefly) known to us, or those who could be consistently identified (such as Q63, or the officer we called "Red Top"). We marked the areas behind the minicab and the police car. Referred to as "white shadows," these areas simulate the shadows that would have been created if the camera had been a powerful light source. We marked these areas red. Thick red lines on the tracking chart indicate when an officer disappeared into this blind zone, from where they could potentially have entered the minicab and retrieved the gun without being seen from Witness B's location.

In total, officers entered the blind zone behind the minicab more than a dozen times. The IPCC's investigators did not examine any of these moments in detail.

If the gun was in fact transported to the grass, it may have required that multiple officers be involved. As such, we also identified in the footage moments of potential "connection" between officers, defined as a point at which two or more moved close enough to one another that an object such as a gun could possibly have been passed between them. Between the blind zone and these connections, we were able to establish a number of potential pathways for the gun to move from the minicab to the grass.

The tracking chart overleaf is not conclusive evidence that the gun was moved by police officers. But it shows the ways it could have been, and demonstrates that, based on the footage alone, the IPCC had no grounds to rule out the possibility that any officers entered the rear of the minicab.

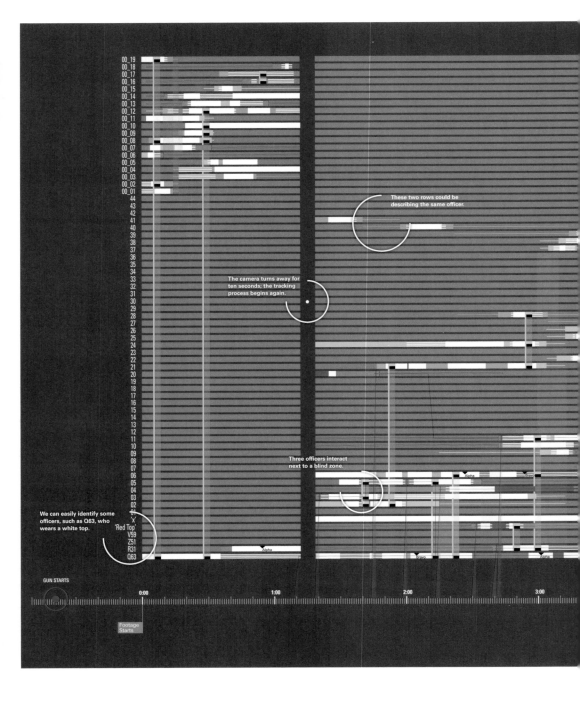

We can easily identify some officers, such as Q63, who wears a white top.

The camera turns away for ten seconds; the tracking process begins again.

Three officers interact next to a blind zone.

These two rows could be describing the same officer.

GUN STARTS

Footage Starts

Diagram charting the movement of every figure visible in Witness B's footage from the moment the clip starts to just after the gun is found, almost eight minutes later. In addition to the thirteen CO19 officers involved in the stop, at least two uniformed officers arrived shortly after the shooting.

Each row corresponds to a visible "figure," though the inability to consistently track some individuals resulted in the chart containing many more rows than there were individuals present at the scene. White rows represent when a figure is visible; colored rows indicate when the figure is partially obscured within a blind zone.

Also indicated are possible "interactions" between officers; between these rows and cross-cutting interactions, purple lines plot dozens of possible routes for the gun to be moved from the minicab to the grass.

The diagram was first shown in this form at the exhibition "War Inna Babylon," which opened at London's Institute of Contemporary Arts in July 2021.

A four-second gap in the footage, which the IPCC's experts missed.

Q63 disappears behind the minicab for twelve seconds.

PC Christiansen
PC Gibson

GUN ENDS

4:00        5:00        6:00        7:00        8:00

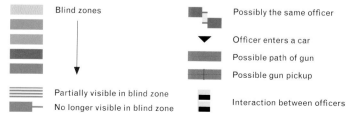

7m38s: the gun is found, according to officers.

Blind zones

Partially visible in blind zone

No longer visible in blind zone

Possibly the same officer

Officer enters a car

Possible path of gun

Possible gun pickup

Interaction between officers

## Chains of Connection

We mapped the dozens of possible
chains of connection by which the
gun could have been carried from the
minicab to the grass.

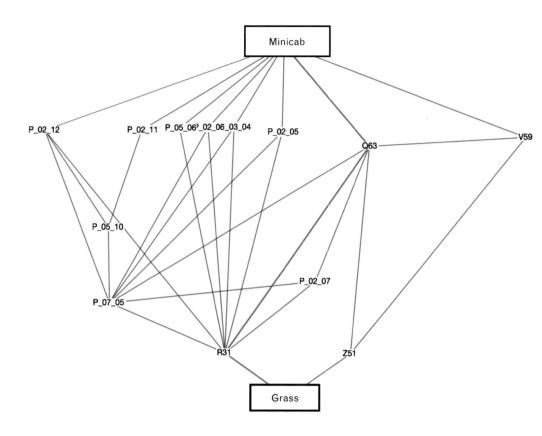

For example: around five minutes into Witness B's clip, Q63 is seen entering the blind zone behind the minicab. He is out of sight in that area for around twelve seconds. Forty seconds later, Q63 passes by R31; they pause for a moment next to one another. Two minutes later, at around seven and a half minutes into Witness B's footage, the gun is reportedly found.

R31 is standing on the green, near its location. Officer Z51 is also nearby. It was these two officers who claimed to have found the gun. They can be seen in a photo taken by a member of the public from the other side of the park.

*Left: Photograph taken by a witness showing officers Z51 and R31 on the grassy area at approximately the time the gun was reportedly found there. Image National Archives.*
*Right: Using the photograph within our model, we matched the position of the officers captured in the photograph with that of the same two officers visible in this area in Witness B's clip. Because the photograph offers a second vantage point on the scene, it allowed us to calibrate more precisely their locations. Matching the locations within the model also helped synchronize the time of the photograph against the timeline of Witness B's footage.*

## The Gap

The IPCC also hired two expert video analysts to study Witness B's clips. But both of them failed to identify and examine a clear "break" in the BBC footage: from one frame to the next, officers are transported from one part of the image frame to another, clearly indicating that a number of frames were not captured. Before the interruption, we see Q63 on the right of the minicab. When the footage begins again, Q63 is on the left. Measuring the speed and timing of other officers, we estimated this gap to be about four seconds in duration. But neither the inquest nor the IPCC noticed this gap, or examined its importance. We tested what could be the source of such a gap by filming a scene on a BlackBerry phone similar to that used by Witness B. We discovered that such gaps are created when the phone receives a call or a text message. We highlighted this finding as part of our effort to convince the Independent Office of Police Complaints to reopen the investigation into Duggan's killing. For it to do so requires "new evidence" to be brought to its attention, and both this "gap" and Bauer's biomechanical study arguably constituted such evidence.

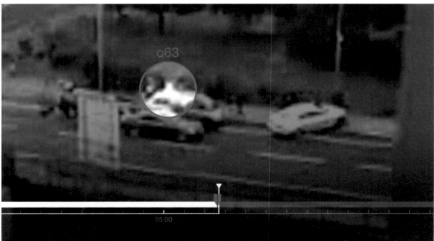

The central question orienting our investigation was: "How did the gun get to the grass?" There were three possible routes. Our analysis shows that the route the IPCC claimed was "most plausible"—that Duggan threw the gun at the time he was shot—is not consistent with the available spatial or biomechanical evidence.

We also show that the route preferred by the inquest jury—that the gun was thrown from the minicab—requires at least four officers with their eyes on Duggan to have missed the gun being thrown. Finally, we demonstrate a number of ways in which the third route—that the gun was planted by police officers—could be plausible, despite both the inquest jury and the IPCC discounting this possibility. ☐

*On 30 November 2019, Forensic Architecture presented the findings
of its investigation to the public for the first time. The event, held at
the old Tottenham town hall, was organized and introduced by
Stafford Scott, founder of Tottenham Rights. Below is an edited
version of his remarks.*

I would like to ask the family of Mark Duggan to make yourselves
known. Don't want to put you on the spot, but we are here for
you guys. [*Applause.*]

We've lost five people at the hands of the state: Cynthia Jarrett,
Joy Gardner, Roger Sylvester, Mark Duggan, and Jermaine Baker.
I would ask that we all have one minute's silence in their memories.

We've lost five to the state, and we do not wish that to happen
to any other community, which is why we are holding this meeting
today. For this is not just about our past, a past which a lot of
you are familiar with; for me, it is about the future. It is about how
we defend our community, how we find new partners as we fight
the state and try to get justice, and how we might save and protect
people going forward.

Most importantly though, it's a meeting for reflection. It's been
a long, long struggle. It started here in Tottenham eight years ago.
Eight years ago, we had meetings in this space, and a crowd packed
out those meetings, and many of those people who were here with
us then are not here with us today, for myriad different reasons.
That's not a criticism of those people; it's an observation. What it
tells us is that the struggle is hard, and it is long, and it is difficult.

And with the Duggan verdict, people say, "What did you expect,
Staff? It's the state protecting the state; what do you expect?"
And I ask them what they expect of me. Because it's the state protecting the state, should I stop campaigning? Should I stop supporting
families in their quest for justice? Should we do what the state
wants us to do and stop using that word "justice"? Because that's
what they want us to do: they want us to stop saying we are going
to fight for justice. I support families because I see what happens to
families in these moments. I see that that one action on that one
day has a ripple effect that goes on for years and sometimes decades.
I've seen it fracture families that used to be solid before. We can't
leave families on their own to take on the weight of the state, because
that's an impossible task.

And I know that you have heard that Mark's family accepted
an out-of-court settlement as a result of mediation recently, but I
want people to understand that that's just kind of a process. It doesn't
mean that our struggle to show people what happened — what we
believe and have always believed happened to Mark Duggan on the
fourth of August in Tottenham — ends with the police paying an

amount of money. Far from it; in some sense, the police paying that money is an acknowledgement from them, for the very first time, of their wrongdoing. The family have done what the family have had to do, and I support them; families are not political, and they should not be expected to be used as battering rams to beat down the doors of the state for us to get justice.

The Duggan family learned about what happened to Mark at the same time that everybody else did. They had to experience their trauma, their heartache, in the full clear light of the public eye. And on the back of it, when some of us went down to Tottenham police station, it kicked off, and then they had to bear the media and the world not just calling their son, nephew, father a gangster, but linking him to the riots that spread throughout the country.

I can't tell you the kind of pressures and strain that were put on the family members, and today I'm here to pay respect to the family, who have fought with dignity at all times regardless of what the media threw at them, regardless of what allegations were made, regardless of how they were treated by the state, and regardless of sitting through three months of an inquest where we had the most perverse verdict ever, I would say.

I want to play you a conversation I had with the Metropolitan Police Service, who contacted me and wanted to ask about today's meeting. [*Scott takes out his phone and plays a recording of the phone conversation with the police officer whose call he was returning.*]

[*Phone rings. The police officer answers and identifies himself.*]
– *Hello, good afternoon, it's Stafford Scott here, sir.*
– *Hello, Stafford. How are you?*
– *Not bad. Yourself?*
– *Not bad, mate. You don't know me from Adam, do you, so I do apologize for ringing you. [He introduces himself.] I know you've got an event on over the weekend in relation to Mark, and I was just wondering whether you would be happy to meet and have a chat?*
– *About what, sir?*
– *Just about the event, and what's sort of planned for it, and how it's going to go.*
– *And why would I want to do that, sir?*
– *Well, I'm just asking if you'd be interested in doing that with me, so that we can sort of support you in any way that you need supporting.*
– *Are you having a laugh?*
– *No.*
– *I'm surprised. I don't understand why you called my phone, to be honest with you. I've run lots of meetings and I never needed the police's support to put on a successful event.*
– *No, I'm sure you don't, but obviously with the history of what went on, we're just a little bit concerned that you've got some support there if you need it.*
– *History of what went on?*
– *With Mr. Duggan, obviously.*

- *You mean the fact that you killed him?*
- *Sorry?*
- *You mean the fact that the police killed him?*
- *Well, I'm not going to go into that level of detail, but it's up to you if you'd like to meet. If you want to have a chat and discuss it, we would be more than happy to do so.*
- *Why would I, sir? Look, if you want to talk about Duggan, alright, one of the things we learned about Duggan, well, not even about Duggan but the riots that took place afterwards [...] is that coppers can't just come into our borough where we live, where we live, and then talk to us about events that we are holding when we don't know you from Adam, as you said at the outset. Why the hell should I talk to you? And why are you even phoning me to discuss what I'm doing? I don't know you.*
- *Okay, well, the offer's there, and if you don't want to meet to discuss this, [...] I'm only offering, that's all.*
- *Yeah, but this ain't how you go about business, is it, sir?*
- *Well, I don't really see what else I can do, other than contact you and hold a discussion with you.*
- *No. What you do is you contact people when you come into their community, you introduce yourself, you say who you are, and you tell us that you're going to give us some fair and just policing. You develop a relationship; you don't just come and ask people about their business. I don't come and ask you about your business, do I, sir? And you're a public servant.*
- *Well, that's the intention of the meeting with you, was to sit down with you and discuss ...*
- *Yes, but why would I? I don't know you from Adam ... [Scott turns off the recording.]*

You get the drift. We are a community that is over-policed; anything we try to do, they are on us. We had those riots that happened in 2011, and the police accept that a significant reason why it happened was a breakdown in the relationship between them and the community. They said that they should engage with us, but they don't engage with us; they police us. Right now you don't see the Mandem in here — those would be Mark's friends, those who come from Broadwater Farm. They don't come and stand and hang with us, because they're facing some of the most oppressive policing that came straight out following the killing of Mark Duggan. They are in the Matrix database; most of them have had to return their licenses to the DVLA [Driver and Vehicle Licensing Agency] because the police have told the DVLA that they should not be driving cars. Information about them is shared with all state agencies, from the benefits office to the housing associations. They are facing the most oppressive kinds of policing, and nothing has changed in this borough since August 2011, when they took the life of Mark Duggan.

Now, many people may think that they know what happened with Mark. Many people may think that they know what took place in the inquest. But the odds are, unless you were there, you really don't know You only know what the media told you. We learned a lot of things through that three-month inquest: one thing we learned is that when you go into these situations you do not have parity of arms; we had one QC, they had about ten. Every police officer had their own QC. There's no fairness, there's no parity. And in this inquest, above everything we had RIPA, the Regulation of Investigatory Powers Act, which meant that we couldn't have a coroner do the inquest; we had to have a judge, who had secret evidence that none of us were ever able to have access to. We had a judge, Judge Keith Cutler — and I don't often say this about judges — who appeared to be an actual gentleman, who wanted to do his job and find the truth, but we could see that he had to keep some things to himself. Only he could hear certain information. We knew that during the court case. What we didn't know was this: during the court case, he heard information about how the police operate, about Trident processes. He knew things we didn't know. He had a counsel in his court who supposedly represented him, meaning the counsel would question the witnesses on his behalf. Now get this: the counsel would question the witness on his behalf, and if the witness — the witness would be the police — lied to the counsel, the judge might know, but he can't tell his counsel that he knows that the police are lying. That means that he can't tell his counsel to pursue and follow and get to the truth.

In his report, the judge wrote: "I was left with an impression of some uncertainty about precisely what was being investigated, on whose behalf, for what purpose, and by what means."

I say to you today, that Judge Keith Cutler by putting that there, was saying: "If left to me, I could not come out with a finding of lawful killing." It is impossible for him to utter those words and come out with the finding that that jury did. We said on the day that the jury's finding was perverse, and we say it today that the jury's finding was perverse.

So now I am going to back off. You see what the judge says; he says I don't know what was going on in that crime scene. The only people who really know were the police officers there, and these people sitting here. Let me introduce you to Forensic Architecture.

If there is an undercover in here — if there isn't, I'll be really disappointed — I say, go back to your bosses and tell them that the payout isn't the end; the payout was an acknowledgement that it was your mistake. That is how we see it in Tottenham; an admission of guilt. We are not done; it is not over. We are not going to make no promises about justice. There is no such thing as *justice*; what we know is that there is *just us*, and on the 4th of August 2011, there literally was just us, right by your house, and the world was against us.

But today is a different story; we have changed the minds of many people. This will help to make up the minds of many people, all those youths who came after. You ask any young Black kid, especially those born in any part of London, what happened to Mark Duggan, and they'll tell you, they believe that they saw him executed, and you can't tell them different. So we are winning; we're winning the minds, the hearts, and the eyes of people. There's us, there's Grenfell, there's Derry, there's Hillsborough; there's more and more of us coming together, more and more of us being forced awake. People say we can't make a difference; well, they're wrong. If we believed that and if it was true, I would be talking to you as an enslaved person. We made a difference then, and we made a difference in South Africa. Let no one tell you we can't make a difference. As a matter of fact, when they tell you that you can't make a difference, you tell them that Stafford Scott said this: The problem isn't the state; the state is doing what the state does. The problem is them, the ones who know and are telling you that you can't make a difference because they are sitting on the fence. Martin [Luther King] had enough quotes about people who sit on the fence, but I will end with this one: "Can't make a difference? Then I'll die trying." If you live a life where you can't find something that is worth dying for, then you haven't lived a life at all. Love and respect; thanks for coming. Tell people what you saw here today. □

A few days after the first public presentation of our investigation in November 2019, *The Guardian* carried a report on our findings, and in February 2020, the IOPC accepted our invitation to visit our offices to discuss the case. There, the IOPC's most senior lawyer, David Emery —who had worked on the original report on the Duggan shooting— had the opportunity to experience the incident from the perspective of V53 within our immersive virtual reality reconstruction. Shortly after the visit, we wrote to the director of the IOPC with a formal request that they reopen the original IPCC investigation.

More than a year later, in May 2021, we received a letter from Sal Naseem, the IOPC's regional director for London, with a final decision regarding our request. "Following the initial assessment," he wrote, "I was satisfied that the information provided gave sufficient reasons to believe that compelling reasons to re-investigate may apply. It was therefore necessary to move to the formal 'review' stage of the re-opening process." Though we had not been informed of this turn of events, we had already inferred that this might be the case given the slow response of the IOPC. Coupled with the Metropolitan Police's agreement to a financial settlement with the family, the delayed response had given us hope that a decade after the shooting of Duggan, the police watchdog might finally be willing to address the police's racialized brutality and to work toward reversing the characterization of Duggan's death as a "lawful killing."

The May 2021 letter continued, however, to outline why the IOPC had finally decided that Forensic Architecture's work did not meet the primary condition for reopening such a case, namely whether there is "anything in the new reports that suggest [the IOPC's] findings were incorrect or that undermine our findings?" Misrepresenting some of our evidence and ignoring crucial elements of our findings and of the expert reports we had drawn on, Naseem wrote that "after careful consideration it is my decision that it is not appropriate to re-investigate this matter."[1]

In response, the lawyers for the Duggan family stated: "The family of Mark Duggan are disappointed and saddened—if not entirely surprised— to see the shabby response from the IOPC to cogent new evidence presented by Forensic Architecture. Unfortunately, it appears that the courage required to confront and follow up the implications of that evidence remains signally lacking in the IOPC today, just as its predecessor body—the IPCC—failed to do its job at every stage since Mark was shot dead almost ten years ago. Like the IPCC, the IOPC seems unable or unwilling to fulfil its responsibilities in relation to contentious deaths at the hands of the police. The consequence is not just that the IOPC lack the confidence of Mark's family and that of other families in their position; the ultimate casualty is the rule of law itself, which depends upon those who enforce the law being seen to be answerable to the law: that is patently not what we can see in the case of Mark Duggan." ☐

1. Our detailed response to the IOPC rebutting their claims, as well as all other correspondence with them, is available on the Forensic Architecture website at <bit.ly/3pxUNkj>.

**The Police Shooting of Mark Duggan**

Editors:
Sina Najafi
Eyal Weizman

Associate Editor:
Jeffrey Kastner

Assistant Editors:
Elizabeth Breiner
Robert Trafford

Proofreaders:
Julianna Bjorksten
Xiran Lu

Graphic Designer:
Stuart Bertolotti-Bailey

**Investigation by
Forensic Architecture**

Principal Investigator:
Eyal Weizman

Researcher-in-Charge:
Christina Varvia

Project Coordinators:
Nicholas Masterton
Robert Trafford

Research:
Martyna Marciniak
Tom James

Video Editing:
Antoine Schirer

Virtual Reality Design:
Alican Aktürk

Research Assistance:
Lola Conte
Sophie Dyer

Project Support:
Sarah Nankivell

Voiceover:
Kamara Scott

Sound Design:
Odinn Ingibergsson

**Forensic Architecture Reports**

Series editor: Eyal Weizman

ISBN: 978-1-932698-85-5

Printed in Germany by
DZA Druckerei zu Altenburg
GmbH.

Published by Cabinet Books
and the ICA.

Cabinet Books
Immaterial Incorporated
181 Wyckoff Street
Brooklyn, NY 11217
USA
<www.cabinetmagazine.org>

Institute of Contemporary Arts
12 Carlton House Terrace
London SW1Y 5AH
UK

One of the photographs that the Daily Mail and other tabloids used
to illustrate their articles on Duggan showed him looking at the
camera with a menacing, hard-faced expression, befitting his
racialized characterization as a "gangsta" and implying that his death
was justified. The portrait was in fact made by cropping a photograph
of Duggan at his daughter's funeral so that the cemetery setting
and the heart-shaped memorial stone he is holding in his hands were
no longer visible. The expression on Duggan's face was not one of
menace; it was grief.